# CRASH!
# COURSE

## John Graham
### Attorney at Law

with Monica Klinkan

# CRASH! COURSE
## A Kodi Press book

Publishing History
Kodi Press trade paperback 1st edition/ August 1995
Kodi Press trade paperback 2nd edition/ March 1996
Kodi Press trade paperback 3rd edition/ October 1999

Library of Congress Catalog Card Number: 94-12045

For information:
Kodi Press
P.O. Box 2428
Kirkland, WA 98083
(800) 422-4610

ISBN 0-9644750-1-4

"Kodi Press" and the logo are registered in the U.S. Patent and
Trademark Office.
Kodi Press, P.O. Box 2428, Kirkland, WA 98083

**YOU'RE PROBABLY READING THIS** book now because you've recently experienced the nerve-jangling terror and stunning impact of an automobile collision. After surviving all that, you may be faced now with some other equally disturbing difficulties. You're suddenly without a car. You're body has been injured. The tasks of managing your care as you make your way to full physical recovery are overwhelming. Temporary or long-term inability to work means no paychecks coming in. Your money woes are mounting.

After an injury-causing accident, wouldn't it be great to have a road map that showed you how to get out of where you *don't* want to be? This is the time when you need step-by-step instructions that tell you how to prepare your insurance claim and successfully negotiate its settlement.

Over the years, I've discovered that *everyone* making an insurance claim needs some guidance. Our law offices have helped many people in Washington state reduce the stress of negotiating a settlement of their personal injury claim and achieve full recovery after an automobile accident. When writing *Crash! Course*, my aim was to combine my many years of professional experiences with my strong personal commitment to full physical and financial recovery in an easy to read, understandable, and helpful guidebook.

*Crash! Course* can be your road map to successful insurance claim negotiations, helping you navigate your own way through the formidable terrain of the insurance industry and circumvent the many obstacles that can keep you from reaching full recovery. It provides the information and the negotiation tools that many people need to effectively, efficiently, and successfully settle their own insurance claim.

Many of the effective negotiating tools that I've learned over the years are contained in this book. If you think you need help beyond what is offered in this book, give us a call. Our goal, both in this book and in our professional practice is to provide everything you need to successfully reach full physical recovery and settle your own insurance claim. Our toll-free number is **(800) 422-4610.** We'll schedule a free consultation at one of our local neighborhood offices near you, and answer any questions you may have about your case.

If you're stranded at the crossroads of confusion following an automobile accident, *Crash! Course* will teach you what you need to know to get back on the road to full recovery. This book puts *you* back in the driver's seat.

Your journey begins here. May it be one to full and successful recovery!

John M. Abraham

# Contents

# Table of Contents

# Table of Contents

# Graham Cracker

"Sure, it's a pain to parallel park, but I dare anyone to rear-end me!"

# Property Damage

If you've been in an automobile accident, count yourself lucky if the only thing damaged was your car. Personal injuries caused by an automobile accident are traumatic, painful, and often very expensive to treat and heal. Damage to your *automobile* can also be traumatic, painful, and expensive to fix! If your car was damaged in an accident, you'll find helpful information in this chapter about your rights and obligations when seeking repair of your car.

Remember, if you've been injured in an accident, your first priority on your road to physical recovery is to get competent medical care. But don't overlook the importance of pursuing and getting maximum reimbursement for damages to your car immediately after the accident. Let's take a look at some of the facts and fiction about what you should and shouldn't do when it comes to getting your damaged car repaired at the insurance company's expense.

*If you are in an accident and you disagree with the other party about who caused the accident, call your attorney immediately. Proving liability is best handled by a trained professional skilled in determining your legal rights and entitlements in situations where liability is in question.*

## Towing

Who pays when your car needs to be towed after being damaged in an accident by a negligent driver? If you were injured in the accident and incapable of driving your car away from the scene, it was probably towed to the nearest wrecking yard. Perhaps your car was so heavily damaged that it was rendered inoperable. In either case, you are faced with what can become sizable charges for towing and storage. Let's talk about who is responsible for paying for what, and how you go about making sure that you are reimbursed for any towing and storage expenses.

Who eventually ends up paying depends on proving *liability* — who was at fault in the accident. If a party breaches any legal duty, that party may be "liable." In this book, we are going to assume that you were the damaged party and that another driver was the negligent party, or at fault, in the accident, and hence is responsible for your losses. Unfortunately, many auto accidents are caused by actions and circumstances that can lead to frustrating, protracted battles over proving who's at fault. Sometimes these cases become complex early on. When that happens, the likelihood of your obtaining a speedy reimbursement for your out-of-pocket towing and storage expenses from the other party's insurance carrier diminishes as the duration of the battle lengthens.

Sometimes, your car will be towed more than once, from the scene of the accident to a wrecking yard, and then from the wrecking yard to a body shop. Towing charges add up, and if your car sits in the wrecking yard for any period of time, storage charges will also grow as each day ticks by.

You may be reimbursed by several sources, including your own insurance company, the negligent party's insurance company, or the negligent party.

If your car is towed, you are responsible for the towing bill. The towing company that takes your car from the scene of the accident will look to you for payment. When you go to the storage yard to retrieve your car, you will be asked to pay all the charges in full — and usually in cash — before you can have your car. You must then look to your insurance company or the negligent driver's insurance company for reimbursement. If you have to pay to have your car towed, the negligent driver or their insurance company must reimburse you for those expenses.

If you are injured in the accident and are unable to drive, or if your car can not be driven because of extensive damage, your insurance company will often arrange to have your car towed to a repair shop. The repair shop will then add that towing bill to your repair bill, and it will become part of the charges reimbursed by the insurance company after your car is repaired.

In a perfect world, the other driver would be clearly negligent and have insurance, and you also would have insurance. In this situation, you have the choice of requesting either your insurance company or the negligent driver's insurance company to reimburse you for all out-of-pocket towing and storage expenses.

If there is some debate as to negligence and liability, you may be cooling your heels for a good long time as the various parties sort through the facts of the accident. If this is the case, you should immediately request that *your* insurance company pay for towing, storage, and rental car expenses. You don't want to wait for a determination of liability while the storage fees add up and you are left without adequate substitute transportation.

Call your insurance company and make an accident report. Ask the important questions. Do I have rental car reimbursement? Do I have collision coverage? Even if I'm at fault, am I covered? Will I be reimbursed for towing charges? If you have adequate coverage, your agent will begin the process of protecting you and providing reimbursement for your losses.

If you don't have adequate coverage, you'll unfortunately find out now why you *should* have had it. While the other driver's insurance company is taking time to evaluate the accident and make a determination of liability, you will be left holding what can turn out to be a very costly bag of costs and expenses that would have been easily handled by your insurance company if you had obtained adequate coverage in the first place.

Washington law requires all drivers to carry a minimum amount of automobile insurance. After an automobile accident, you will likely deal with two insurance companies — yours, and that of the negligent driver. Often, one of the insurance companies will want to have your car towed from the storage facility to its own appraisal facility or to a repair shop of its choice to examine and evaluate the damage to your car. The negligent driver is responsible for towing charges incurred by the insurance company to conduct a damage appraisal.

If the negligent driver does not have insurance, you will have to go directly to the at-fault driver for reimbursement. This could mean going to court against the negligent driver to obtain reimbursement for your property damage. Your insurance company will reimburse you, then file a lawsuit against the negligent driver for repayment of the money it paid you.

## Storage

Once your car has been towed to a storage facility, daily charges begin to add up. The negligent driver is responsible for reimbursing you for all storage charges, from the time of the accident to the time the insurance company authorizes release of your car for repairs.

**If you postpone repair of your car because of a dispute with the insurance company, you may be held personally liable for any storage expenses incurred. The law requires you to reasonably *mitigate*, or lessen, your own damages. You can't abandon your car for three months at the storage yard and expect the insurance company to compensate you for the charges.**

The insurance company is obligated to act in "good faith." In the State of Washington, "bad faith" is the absence of good faith. It doesn't necessarily mean that the insurance company has to show ill will, or a determined effort to make your life miserable as you attempt to settle the claim. It does mean that the insurance company, and its employees and agents, must work with due diligence to settle your claim responsibly and expeditiously. They must provide a fair market value replacement for all of your losses to make you "whole" again, that is, as you were before the accident.

*You also have a common law duty to act in good faith. This means that you are to act reasonably and not exaggerate, lie, or fraudulently claim damages. Insurance fraud is a serious offense that may be punishable by fines, incarceration, or both.*

You have the right to remove personal belongings from your car, upon showing proof that you own the car. Sometimes you will be granted ready access to your car accompanied by watchful storage facility employees. They share your concern that valuable items may be removed from your car by unauthorized persons while it is stored on their property.

When you are granted access to your car by the storage facility, it is important that you obtain an accurate, detailed receipt for every item you remove from your car.

---

**Remember that while your car is in storage, daily charges are accumulating. It is important that you or your representative contact the negligent driver's insurance company immediately to make arrangements for the repair of your car. The insurance adjuster is obligated to act in good faith to expeditiously process the towing and repair of your car. It is to your advantage to actively negotiate with the insurance companies, and therefore reduce added storage charges you will be obligated to pay up front.**

---

Let's say that the storage yard was cooperative and let you remove your brand new stereo speakers from your car before your car was towed to the repair shop. Later you are shocked to discover that your valuable seat covers are missing. Without a detailed receipt from the storage yard clearly stating that all you removed was the stereo speakers, you are going to have a hard time proving that you did not also take the seat covers when you were given access to your car.

Sometimes you will be refused access to your car because the facility does not want to assume responsibility for what may happen to your car and to the items and equipment in it. It can be frustrating facing off with a wrecking yard "go-fer" who, with greasy arms firmly crossed, obstinately refuses to allow you to retrieve valuable business papers from your car.

What can you do? Unfortunately, the law is not clear on this issue. Sometimes nothing short of your paying to have your car towed off of their "protected" property and to the repair shop will provide access to your own car. Call the insurance agent handling your claim and request assistance in gaining access to your car.

## Automobile Repairs

You have the right to have your car repaired by *any* body shop you choose. Insurance companies typically avoid any semblance of an affiliation with any one body shop, to avoid being in an uncomfortable position if you discover later that the repairs were inadequate or defective.

Everyone has stories about the "Body Shop Nightmare." If you do not already know of a reputable body shop, check around. Ask your family, friends, and co-workers. Call your own insurance agent, and ask for a recommendation. Call the Better Business Bureau for your area and ask about the reputation of local shops.

Once your car has been delivered to the body shop, you can begin negotiating with the negligent driver's insurance company to decide which insurance company pays for the repairs to your car. If you decide to have your insurance company pay, they will send an adjuster to the repair shop. The adjuster and the repair shop will negotiate appropriate repairs and costs. They compare their evaluations of the damage, and refer to automobile repair guidelines that provide the prevailing rates. The adjuster and the repair shop agree to the appraised charges, and the work is performed on your car.

*Have the insurance company deal directly with the repair shop. This provides an "implied warranty" that the insurance company will back up the body shop and help guarantee that your car is satisfactorily repaired.*

Your insurance company cuts a check directly to the repair shop for the work and for any towing expenses that were "fronted" by the repair shop. Your insurance company will then request and obtain reimbursement from the negligent driver or their insurance company for the cost of repairs to your car.

If you request that the negligent driver's insurance company cover the cost of repairs, they will work with the repair shop to determine a fair repair cost. They will pay the repair shop directly for the repairs to your car.

## Pocketing the Money

In the alternative, you can take your car to several different body shops for estimates. You can submit

9

all of the estimates, or only the highest ones, to the insurance company. They will review the estimates and negotiate with you on the amount of money they will pay for repairs. They will probably send their adjuster out to look at your car and provide their own in-house estimate. When the insurance company writes you the check, you can take your car and the money to the body shop of your choice and have the repairs completed. Or, you can pocket the money and not repair your car at all.

The disadvantage of pocketing the money is that it represents a release by you. You are in essence saying that you've settled your claim for property damage. You are out of luck if you later discover that there is additional, more costly damage to your car that was not included in the settlement. Don't try to work a deal where you pocket the money and repair the car yourself, or have your favorite uncle repair it, or worse yet, not repair it at all. It is to your advantage to take your car in and have it repaired by a reputable body shop that will perform quality work.

## Payment for Repair Charges

The body shop will often coordinate other repairs to your car that can not be made at their facility. If the upholstery has to be cleaned, or the windshield needs replacing, the body shop will coordinate with other businesses to provide these services. They will add their charges to the body shop bill and submit all charges to the insurance company for payment.

The body shop will use factory-new parts if your car is less than three years old. After three years, used parts are customarily used. You may request that only new, "OEM" parts be used to repair your car if it is more than three years old. However, you will pay the cost difference between a used part and a new one.

The "life expectancy" of your car's parts are also factored into the amount of money the insurance company is willing to pay for repairs. For example, if your tires have 20,000 miles of wear, they have already "used up" 50% of their 40,000 mile life expectancy. If they were destroyed in the accident, the insurance company will reimburse you 50% of the tire's life expectancy. The same rule holds for mufflers, brakes, and other parts that customarily wear out over time.

The body shop will typically repaint only those sections of the car that suffered damage. If your car is more than a few years old, you will probably be able to see a difference between new and original paint. Again, you can request that the entire car be re-painted, but you will pay for the difference between painting the damaged sections and painting the whole car. The insurance company is not obligated to pay for repainting undamaged sections of your car.

CONSTRUCTION AHEAD

*All of the charges submitted to the insurance company must be for repair of accident-related damage. The insurance adjuster must be satisfied that the repairs are legitimate before paying for the charges.*

## Taking Delivery of Your Repaired Car

Washington State law requires that your car be in the same condition after repair as it was before the accident. If you find that you car is *not* in the same condition, it will be a bone of contention between you and the paying insurance company. Once the repairs are completed, it is important that you perform a *complete* examination and evaluation of your car *before* accepting delivery of the car.

When faced with a complaint that the car is not properly aligned, or that things "just aren't right," the insurance company will insist that unibody cars are repaired to factory precision, and that your car has been returned to its pre-accident condition. You have the right to obtain the services of a professional automobile appraiser, *at your expense*, to evaluate and document the condition of your car following repair. Such an objective evaluation may be worth the expense if you find yourself in a dispute with the insurance company and the body shop over the quality of the repairs.

It's difficult and sometimes impossible to prove six months down the line that your car's brakes are failing because of damage incurred during the accident, or that your trunk leaks a year later because the seals were broken upon impact. The insurance company will look closely at all opportunities you may have had to discover the problem earlier. Also, it will be your duty to prove to the insurance company or to a court that the cause of the problem was the accident itself. Normal wear and tear, or a pre-existing condition, or another, subsequent accident will quickly reduce your claim for additional damage.

## Repair of Personal Items

You are entitled to retrieve and repair or replace items of personal property that were damaged in the accident. Perhaps your set of golf clubs in the trunk was crushed on impact, or the leather jacket you were wearing was ripped when you struck the steering wheel. The insurance company will want to see proof of the value of such items. A bill of sale is the most convincing proof. If you do not have that, photographs of the items prior to the accident would be most helpful. If you don't have a bill of sale or other reliable documentation, submit a claim for losses of personal items. Negotiate with the insurance company for satisfactory reimbursement for repairs or for the replacement value of the items.

## Rental Car

When your car is damaged and you lose the use of your car, you are entitled by law to a replacement vehicle. The negligent driver is required to either rent a car for you, or pay you for loss of use of your car during the period that your car is disabled. The replacement car does not have to equal your car in value or quality. So, if your brand new Cadillac is sitting in the repair shop awaiting repair, the rental car provided by the insurance company may very well be an economy compact. Typically, you will be reimbursed $16.00 per day for a rental car for the time between when your car was damaged in the accident, and when your car is repaired and returned to its prior condition. You may upgrade your rental car from the model offered at the $16.00 insurance rate, but you are responsible for any increased charges due to the upgrade.

You are required to show proof of automobile insurance when you sign the rental contract. Many rental companies will not rent to minors, and some will not rent to individuals under the age of 25. Also, many rental companies will demand payment by way of a credit card. The insurance company is *not* obligated to provide a rental car if you do not meet the rental contract requirements.

If you do not meet the requirements of the rental agency providing the rental car, you may have someone else rent the car for you and name you on the contract as an authorized driver. Failing that, you may have no choice but to accept the $16 per day payment from the insurance company and to rely on the good graces of friendly drivers, the bus, or your own two feet to get where you need to go.

Many body shops provide rental cars on the premises. When you drop your car off for repair, you can get a rental car right there. When you return to the shop to drop off the rental car and pick up your repaired car, the repair shop will simply add the rental charges onto your bill and the insurance company will write a check for the full amount.

You may not need a rental car while your damaged car is in for repairs. Perhaps you have a second car, or maybe your injuries preclude you from driving while your car is being repaired. You are nevertheless entitled to reimbursement of $16.00 per day during the period that you are without your car. If the insurance company doesn't offer you the reimbursement, speak up and ask for it!

## Total Loss

The determination of "total loss" of your car is far from an exact science. A typical approach is the "70% rule." If your car suffers damages totaling 70% of its value, the insurance company will likely write your car off as a total loss and issue you a check that represents the fair market value of your car before the accident. You sign the car over to the insurance company, which in turn sells it to a salvage yard.

Do you have the right to demand that your car be repaired? Washington law says that the negligent party has to pay to repair the car, or reimburse you the fair market value of the car, whichever is *less*. The law doesn't address the total loss of a car. If your car is worth $10,000, and there is $7,000 worth of damage, the negligent driver has to pay you $7,000 to get your car repaired.

If the insurance company declares your car a total loss, and you still want to keep your car, you can make an offer to the insurance company. Perhaps you would like to cannibalize the car for parts, or attempt to repair the car yourself. You can do that, but you end up effectively "buying" your car from the insurance company. The insurance company will sell you your car for the same price that a salvage yard bids to purchase the wreck. You do have the option of obtaining bids from salvage yards to assist you in negotiating with the insurance company for a fair "purchase price" of the totaled car.

If your car is deemed a total loss, the car's title is changed to reflect that. This is done to protect subsequent purchasers of your car by alerting them to its history of substantial damages.

Let's say your car is valued at $10,000, and the salvage yard offers $3000 for the wreck. If you opt to "buy" your car from the insurance company, they will give you $10,000, minus the $3,000, for a total of $7,000. After you receive your $7,000, you are responsible for towing the car to your chosen destination, paying any storage costs, and repairing or disposing of the car.

The no-hassle approach, of course, is to accept a check for $10,000 from the insurance company, turn the car over to them, cash the check, and go buy yourself a replacement car.

## Diminution in Value

Washington law says that the negligent driver has to pay for the *diminution*, or decrease, in value to your car, even though it has been repaired. You've paid $3,000 for repairs to your car, and now the car is worth less than it was before, because it was damaged in the accident.

The insurance company will refer to any one of a number of "Blue Books" to determine an appropriate valuation for your car. Keep in mind that insurance adjusters will generally select the *lowest* valuation for your car. They will refer to the listing for the same make, model, year, and mileage as your car, and offer you a "fair market value" based on the listed information.

How do you go about proving that there has been a diminution, or reduction, in the value of your car? There are two primary determinations to be made: the value of your car *immediately before the accident*, and the value of your car *immediately after repairs*.

How do you prove the value of your car before the accident? If you are one of the rare people who has a long history of repairs of your car by one reputable repair shop, you can have them examine your car and attest to its condition prior to the accident. Most repair shops are not enthusiastic about doing this, because it's very difficult to accurately assess the exact condition of a car just prior to the moment of impact in an accident.

If you can afford to, you can hire an ***independent appraiser*** to evaluate your car and provide a fair market value. The appraiser will examine your car, evaluate the present market, look at comparable sales, and most importantly, determine the value of your car before the accident. Many insurance companies use independent appraisers in their own valuations, and an appraiser's report could provide helpful to your case.

## Document Everything!

Your negotiations will be more effective when you can produce recent repair bills, photographs of your car, and letters and documentation from auto dealers attesting to the market value of your car or similar cars of like make, model, mileage, and condition. Look in recent issues of the *Auto Trader* and other regional automobile classified ads for comparisons and valuations of cars like yours. You will need to determine the asking price, and most importantly, the selling price. Call some of the people who have advertised a car like yours and ask them how much they got for the car.

Write down all the information you gather, make photocopies, collect every document you can get your hands on, and take your case to the insurance adjuster. You'll often find that when presented with convincing documentation, insurance adjusters are willing to re-evaluate their first offer and come up with a figure that may be more acceptable to you. The adjuster wants to settle your claim as quickly as possible for the least amount of money. When you do the legwork for the adjuster and provide convincing documentation that shows a higher valuation for your car, chances are you'll receive a higher payment. It's definitely worth the time and effort to negotiate with documentation in hand if you encounter an unsatisfactory first offer from the adjuster.

Will you ever get "full value" for your damaged car? Not likely. If you just bought a brand new car, drove it off the lot, and got creamed at the next intersection, it is highly unlikely that you will receive the full amount of money that you paid the dealer just moments before the accident. Your car depreciated dramatically in value from the moment you first started the engine and drove it off the dealer's lot. Most of us pay an inflated price for the cars we buy from a dealer. That's the nature of the car business. And the insurance company is not about to accept your arguments that what you paid for the car is equal to the actual fair market value of the car. You may have paid $18,000 for that sporty little beauty, but the insurance company will counter with a $14,000 fair market valuation. You probably won't be able to boost that seemingly low valuation any higher.

 **What if you don't agree with the insurance company's valuation? You can negotiate with the insurance company. When your car is involved in a damaging accident, there are two very important things to remember when negotiating with the in-surance company for a fair reimbursement: negotiate *in person*, and provide ample *documentation*.**

## Summary

After an automobile accident, attending to the repair or replacement of your car often seems like the most important thing you need to do. It's amazing how quickly we feel helpless and stranded without our trusted car in one piece and parked conveniently in the garage! In this chapter, we covered what you need to do immediately after an automobile accident to ensure that your car and your personal possessions are returned to you, or replaced, so that you are in the same condition after the accident as you were before.

The most important thing you need to remember, and the most important job you need to accomplish after an automobile accident, is devoting all of your energies to *full physical recovery*. While it may seem that the only thing you really want and need right now is to get your car back, return to work, and get your life back on track, none of these things is going to be possible or even of any use to you if you do not have the good health and physical ability to enjoy them.

If you've been injured in an automobile accident, wait until you've sufficiently recovered before you attempt to solve all of the hassles involved in getting your car repaired or replaced. Now that you know what needs to be done to obtain full compensation for damages to your car, you, or a trusted family member or friend who steps in on your behalf, can ensure that the damages to your car are satisfactorily handled by your insurance company. Or you can ask an attorney to represent you and handle all of the details of your claim.

Whomever you choose to oversee the repair or replacement of your car, nothing is more important than your physical recovery. Your car and your other material possessions are replaceable. That's why you have automobile insurance! Your health and well-being, on the other hand, are far more fragile and can't be replaced with a check from the insurance company. Physical recovery demands a great degree of vigilant care and protection on your part. That's why we'll be talking a little later in this book about maximizing your physical recovery.

## Survival Guide Checklist

☐  Your physical recovery is your top priority!

☐  Work with the system to get you car repaired the right way, the first time.

☐  **Document! Document!! Document!!!**

☐  Get photos of your damaged car.

☐  Negotiate in person.

☐  Know your consumer rights.

# NOTES

# Understanding Insurance Coverages

When was the last time you asked yourself, "What insurance do I have?" Better yet — when was the last time you were able to *answer* that question? Unfortunately, too often folks find that they know little or nothing about the policies they've purchased to insure their health, automobiles, homes, businesses, and even their credit cards, in the event of loss, damage, or injury.

Now that you need to use that automobile insurance policy, do you even know what it does and doesn't cover? If you're like most people, you probably don't. Most of us buy insurance because we know it's the right and prudent thing to do. We depend on our agent to make many of our choices, hopefully in our best interest. But when the time comes to make a claim against a policy, or multiple policies, too often we find ourselves asking all the questions then that we should have asked when we first signed on the dotted line.

This chapter will give you the information you need to investigate all of your insurance options, and equip you with the knowledge and facts that you need to claim all of the benefits to which you are legally entitled. You'll learn how to:

- Identify all available insurance payment sources.
- Know what to look for in an insurance policy.
- Submit your bills to the appropriate insurer.
- Pursue full payment of your claims.

## Asking the Right Questions

Am I covered for all accidents? What if I'm physically injured? What if the accident was my fault? And what about towing? What if I'm unable to work because of my injuries? How am I going to pay my personal bills and the mortgage? How much will the policy pay? Can my insurance company refuse to pay for medical care? How long will payments continue after the accident? Who should I turn to for payment — my own insurance policy ("first party insurance"), or the other driver's policy ("third party insurance")?

What is "full coverage"? If you have liability, uninsured and underinsured motorist coverage, collision, comprehensive, towing, rental car, and PIP coverage, you are probably adequately covered. However, review your policy yearly to make sure the policy limits are keeping up with inflation and your own minimum financial needs should you require the benefits of your insurance policy after an automobile accident and disabling injury.

The answers to these questions about coverage and limits are always determined by (1) the actual language in the policy, (2) whether the policy was in force at the time of the accident, (3) the case law (previous legal rulings that have been made in similar situations), (4) other statutes and laws, and (5) the facts of the accident.

**A competent attorney will provide a preliminary review of your case at no cost. He'll advise you of the merits of your claim, and whether he can help you or if you can easily settle the claim on your own. Call an attorney specializing in personal injury, and ask if an initial consultation is free. Those thirty free minutes could determine the dif-ference between $500 in your pocket and $5,000.**

Some of your questions can bring surprising answers. If you've shopped wisely for insurance *before* the accident, and are willing to invest some time and effort *after* the accident to research the insurance coverage that is available to you, you may be pleasantly surprised when the time comes to review your options for reimbursement.

On the other hand, if you have inadequate or nonexistent insurance coverage, or if you do not thoroughly research your coverage options, you may be needlessly saddled with bills and expenses that will grow incrementally until your claim is settled a few years down the road.

How do you best arm yourself with full protection if you've had an accident? First, know your own insurance coverage. Second, discover the insurance coverage of every other party involved in the accident. This will take no small amount of time and effort on your part, but the long-term financial paybacks are well worth the short-term hassle of scrambling for copies of policies from all of the insurance companies involved.

## Identifying Available Insurance Policies

Let's first take a look at some of the more common sources of insurance coverage, and review the best ways for you to reap maximum benefits under these policies. Then, we'll talk about a few of the less common sources of insurance coverage. These can be surprisingly lucrative cash sources that most people don't even think about in their frantic search for reimbursement after a traumatic automobile accident. It's much better to know about and tap all of your resources *now*, rather than face the disappointment *later* of getting too little, or nothing at all.

Your physical recovery is the most important goal throughout any settlement negotiation. Your financial recovery is important, too, but what is financial health without the physical ability to enjoy it? Be especially aggressive about submitting claims for medical care. Your physical recovery *today* has a profound effect on the quality of your life in the future.

## Where to Begin Looking?

After the automobile accident, you need to look at all possible sources of insurance coverage. You should typically look first to the vehicles involved in the accident, and then to the people themselves. This means that you should first investigate the insurance policies covering the at-fault driver's car, then pursue coverage under your own automobile policy. The next step is to review any insurance policies covering both drivers.

Let's start with automobile-related insurance policies, then move on to policies that insure people.

## PIP

Personal Injury Protection ("PIP") coverage is a limited contract between you and your insurance company stating certain benefits that you will receive if you or family members or passengers in your car were injured in an accident, no matter who was at fault. PIP benefits may include payment for lost wages, medical bills, loss of services, home nursing care, even death and funeral benefits. Surprisingly, this outstanding coverage is one of the least expensive options on an insurance policy. It costs little to purchase, and if you have an accident and make a claim against your PIP policy, your insurance company must begin paying you immediately.

Beginning immediately after the accident, you may begin drawing on your PIP benefits to pay for hospital, Chiropractic, and certain out-of-pocket expenses. PIP pays a flat percentage of your normal wages, or up to a maximum weekly amount, beginning on the fifteenth day following your accident.

Please see Chapter 3, *"Personal Injury Protection"* for additional information about this valuable insurance coverage resource.

## Liability Coverage

The State of Washington passed legislation in the 1980's that requires all Washington motorists to carry minimum liability coverage of $25,000 per person. The fines and penalties for failing to have insurance while operating a motor vehicle are extremely high. If you are involved in an automobile accident, and you do not have insurance, you will automatically be fined. If you are at fault, you may lose your driver's license for up to three years, or until you have made full financial reparations to any injured parties.

The law also requires insurance companies to offer uninsured motorist ("UM") and under-insured motorist ("UIM") coverage to every person purchasing liability coverage. An insured who chooses not to purchase UM or UIM coverage must decline the offer in writing.

---

**Both UM (uninsured motorist) and UIM (under-insured motorist) coverage is provided to the policy holder by an insurance company. If your policy includes this coverage, you can submit a claim to your insurance company.**

---

A driver is classified as "uninsured" when he or she injures another party in an accident and has no insurance to cover the damage caused. If you are damaged by such a negligent party, or "tortfeasor," your UM coverage will kick in and pay for damage that you suffered at the hands of the uninsured driver.

An "under-insured" driver is one who has liability insurance, but whose insurance policy limits do not cover the total damage incurred by the injured party. If you incur damages by the negligent acts of an under-insured motorist, you can receive payments for your damages from UIM coverage included in your insurance policy.

UM and UIM coverage can be a financial lifesaver if you are involved in an accident and your damages exceed the available maximum amounts payable under the other driver's insurance policy. For example, if the other driver's policy has a $25,000 payout limit, and your damages and injuries total $65,000, the UM or UIM coverage on *your* policy may kick in and pay the additional costs up to the maximum amount provided by your coverage.

## Business-Related Insurance

If either of the drivers was operating a vehicle while on the job, or if the car is owned by a business, then employer-provided insurance should be investigated. Check into any insurance provided by union membership, employee associations, or professional memberships. Also, if the accident occurred on business premises or because of action by a representative of a business, business liability policies should also be examined for potential coverage.

## Health Insurance

Your health insurance policy is a primary place to look if you are injured in an automobile accident and do not have medical benefits available on your automobile policy. Your health insurance carrier may pay for treatment of injuries and, depending on your policy, may pay for additional treatments, physical therapy, in-home nursing, medical equipment, prescriptions, and the like. After you settle your claim with the at-fault driver, your health insurer may demand reimbursement from the third-party insurance company.

## Homeowner's Insurance

Homeowner's insurance is another potential source of insurance coverage. The language of the policy must be carefully reviewed to identify those clauses that may provide payment for damage, loss, or injury caused by an automobile accident. Many people erroneously assume that "home-owner's" means the accident or injury must occur within the insured home. This may not be true in your case, and the homeowner's policy will reveal if your accident is covered.

## Credit Disability

You will also want to look at any insurance policies that you purchased for your credit cards. Many retailers and auto lenders provide disability or unemployment coverage on major purchases, and automatically bill a monthly premium for this coverage on your credit statement. These policies make minimum payments on the outstanding balance on your account if you are unable to work and pay your bills, keeping your credit history good.

## Mortgage Disability

Do you have disability coverage on your mortgage? Lending institutions customarily offer such coverage. If you are disabled or otherwise prevented from making your mortgage payments, the insurance policy steps in and continues to make mortgage payments to the bank while you cannot. It's important to submit a claim as soon as possible on a mortgage disability policy, so that you can take full advantage of any time or payment limitations provided by your contract, and avoid the financial and emotional trauma of possible mortgage default and foreclosure.

## Other Insurance Options

We've discussed *your* insurance policies, and the policies of the *at-fault driver*. You mustn't overlook another potential source of payment: the policies of spouses, family members, and associates of yours and of the tortfeasor. Also, you should investigate the insurance policies covering any person or entity whose action or inaction may be negligent. Perhaps the failure of a piece of equipment caused the accident, or there was a preventable hazard on the road due to faulty road design, missing road signs, or inadequate lighting. These *contributing* factors could have been contributed by an individual, a business, or a government entity. You will need to look at the "big picture" and identify who, if anyone, may have contributed to your accident.

If any other party or entity breached either a statutory or common law duty, and that breach was a contributing factor to the accident, the insurance policies covering that party may be subject to your claim for damages.

How do you know if one of these insurance policies will reimburse you for damages? First, you need to look at the policy itself. *Do not depend on*

*Always review your own policy for language that supports your claim for payment.*

34

*the insurance agent representing the policy holder*
*to advise you if the policy will cover the accident!*

You should not rely solely on the representations of an insurance agent, adjuster, supervisor, or underwriter. The final determination is found in the insurance policy itself. Only by reading the actual insurance policy can you successfully claim that you should be covered, and to what extent.

Contrary to what it may say in the marketing brochure, your own insurance agent may not be entirely committed to your best interests. Your agent is obligated to keep the cost of doing business — and that includes payments to you — to a minimum.

If you don't receive a response to your request, you have some options. First, be a "squeaky wheel" and make repeated and regular requests, both on the phone and *in writing.* Second, contact the Washington State Insurance Commission and file a formal complaint. Third, contact your attorney and ask him or her to step in. That often produces an *immediate* response.

If you ask the other party for a copy of their insurance policy, your request may be ignored or refused outright. If this happens, call their insurance carrier directly and inform them that you are taking action against their insured and want a *certified* copy of the insurance policy *or policies* covering their insured.

## Policy Review Checklist

Once you get the policy, read all of the language contained in the policy and determine the following:

❏ Is the policy current?

❏ Was the policy in force on the date of the accident?

❏ Is the policy enforceable in the State of Washington?

❏ Does the policy cover the tortfeasor and/ or me?

❏ Are the circumstances of my accident covered by the policy?

❏ If I am at fault, does the policy still cover me?

❏ What will the policy pay for? (For example, lost wages, hospitalization, long-term disability.)

❏ What are the payout limits of the policy?

❏ Are there any time limitations, and should claims be submitted immediately?

❏ How and to whom do I submit claims under the policy?

Once you've identified additional tortfeasors and determined that their insurance covers your accident, you will need to prove that their negligence contributed to the accident and to your injuries. This will likely mean taking the tortfeasor and their insurance company to court.

> Be forewarned! Some insurance policies contain *thousands* of pages in bound book form. The process of translating voluminous insurance policies is unpleasant at best, and sometimes impossible. Consider consulting with an attorney if you find yourself faced with the awesome task of deciphering reams of insurance industry "legalese."

You may often be able to successfully negotiate a settlement with an insurance company for payments from the at-fault driver's policy. However, if you are making claims against multiple tortfeasors for negligent acts that contributed to your damages, the intricacies and demands of negotiation, litigation, and a potential jury trial may pose a challenge well beyond your abilities and resources. Consult an attorney if any of the following apply:

1. You are making claims against more than one party.

2. Negotiations with the insurance company are stalled.

3. You are faced with a courtroom trial.

## Determining Coverage for Injuries

If you're injured in an automobile accident, you typically look to the liability coverage in the at-fault driver's policies and to the UM/UIM and PIP coverage in your own policy. These cover all of your expenses or damages to put you back in the position you would have been in had you not been

*You are entitled to recover for "intangible" damages — pain and suffering, plus any future damages to your physical and financial health.*

37

injured. Items covered include medical bills, wage loss, out-of-pocket expenses, vocational retraining, general damages to cover your pain and suffering, and any other incidental expenses whether they exist now or are likely to arise in the future.

## Stacking Insurance Policies

Most people assume that they must choose between one policy or another when submitting claims for damages. However, in the State of Washington, it is legal to stack insurance policies. This means that you can submit the *same* claim to more than one insurance policy, and receive payment for the claim from *each* insurer.

Some insurance policies contain language that prohibits stacking. Read every policy carefully before purchasing it, and know the rights and benefits to which you are entitled.

Stacking can be compared to buying multiple life insurance policies. These policies provide payment in the event of the death of the insured. Upon death, each policy will pay the stated benefit. It's no different with other insurance policies. You pay an insurance company to provide benefits in case of certain events. If you choose to pay more than one insurance company to cover you for loss, damage, or injury, you are entitled to receive the policy benefits from *each* insurance company if something bad happens.

If you are covered by multiple policies, prioritize the policies based on the size and extent of available benefits. Identify the policy with the most comprehensive, maximum coverage and submit your claims to that carrier first. Then, continue through the remaining policies and submit your claims in an order of priority that exhausts all available benefits. This process of prioritizing all available policies, called *stacking*, will provide you with maximum benefits and the opportunity to fully exercise your rights as an insured.

Insurance laws vary from state to state. Insurance stacking is legal in the State of Washington, but may not be in other states.

Stacking insurance policies can create coverage and billing nightmares. If you decide to retain an attorney to represent you, their office will handle all of the billing procedures, questions, and disputes for you.

## When the Insurance Company Is Slow to Pay

Unlike some other states, Washington has no laws on the books that penalize an insurance company for damages incurred because it was slow in paying, or failed to pay on a claim. Many insurance companies have a policy of delaying payment as long as possible. They can hold onto their cash and earn interest on it as they delay paying you. More importantly, they can often wear you down to the point where you drop your claim all together.

The consumer is left with the short end of the stick in these situations. Even if lack of payment by an insurance company causes you to default on your mortgage, lose your business, or fail to receive necessary medical treatment, you may not be able to claim any additional damages because of the financial and emotional harm caused by the insurance company's actions. If you take an insurance company to court for these reasons, you may only be able to claim the actual amounts that should have been paid in the first place.

## Determining Liability

The process of determining liability is a complex web of fact and circumstance. We can't adequately cover all of the issues of determining liability within the limited scope of this book. In short, *liability*, or who was at fault for an accident, must first be determined before most insurance benefits can be paid.

If the insurance policy is a "no fault" policy, you are paid regardless of liability. A good example of a no fault policy is the typical health insurance policy. If you get hurt, regardless of the reason, your medical costs are covered. Most policies (automobile, homeowners, and the like) are "at fault" policies, which means that liability must be determined *before* benefits are paid.

The determination of fault can take months or even years and can ultimately end up in court. If your accident is not a cut-and-dried case of someone clearly doing something that caused damage, loss, or injury to you, you may well encounter liability issues and denial of damages.

Always assume that the insurance company will attempt to assign fault to someone *other* than its insured. Remember that insurance companies are in business to *make* money, not pay it out to you or anyone else. Police accident reports, eyewitness testimony, photographs, and other exhaustive documentation may be necessary to prove that someone else was at fault.

Unfortunately, the final proof of liability is often only made successfully in court. When dealing with an insurance company on issues of liability, be prepared to take your case to court.

*Are liability issues stalling payment of your claims? Then it may be time to call your attorney, who can help expedite payment of your claims by the insurance company without a prolonged, costly courtroom battle.*

## Negotiating with the Key Players

When submitting a claim for payment to an insurance company, your typical front-line contact will be the insurance agent, either yours or that of other parties to the accident. The agent takes your report and submits your claim to the claims department. Once your claim lands there, you will be dealing with a claims adjuster. This individual "adjusts" how much money you are entitled to, based on the circumstances of the accident and the policy coverage. The adjuster may need to confer with the underwriting department, the folks who actually write the policies and determine coverage parameters.

If the agent or the adjuster is not able to answer your questions or respond to your requests satisfactorily, you may contact the underwriting department directly. However, be advised that you will typically get the same information, and hear the same determinations, from all of these individuals. They are, after all, working for the same company that is determined to hold onto its cash reserves.

Throughout every step of your claim, you must (1) provide complete documentation supporting your claim and (2) negotiate with the insurance company in person. As the injured party making a claim, the burden rests on *you* to prove what you are entitled to.

If you feel that the insurance company is not acting in good faith, contact the Washington State Insurance Commission and make a formal complaint. Be aware that if there is an investigation, it can continue over a long period of time and may not provide a finding on your behalf. If you want a more immediate response from an insurance company, call your attorney.

## Insurance Reimbursement

When you successfully settle your claim with the responsible party's insurer (the third party insurer), they will issue you a check for the settlement amount. Your own insurer will typically make a claim against that third party insurer, and against any settlement paid to you. Your insurer will seek reimbursement of any amounts they paid to you for accident-related losses.

*Even if you think your case is "too small" to merit the involvement of an attorney, think again.*

Let's say the accident caused you to incur $10,000 in medical bills. You used a combination of your automobile PIP coverage and health insurance to pay these bills. You then successfully sued the negligent driver for $25,000. Your own insurance policies likely contain language that obligates you to repay the $10,000 your insurance companies paid on your behalf while you were negotiating a settlement with the third-party insurer.

Are you always obligated to pay your insurance company the full $10,000? Not necessarily. It depends on the amount of coverage the at-fault driver has, and the language in your own policies. You may be able to negotiate the amount of money your insurance company expects to be repaid. If you pursued and successfully managed to obtain a settlement from the third-party insurer, you should be entitled to some benefit for obtaining reimbursement for your first-party insurer.

Negotiating a reduction in the amount due to your insurer can be tricky. Read your policy carefully and know your obligations. Negotiating with facts in hand and dogged determination may increase the settlement moneys that land in your own pocket.

Insurance companies are not enthusiastic about negotiating with their policy holders to reduce the amount of money they expect to be reimbursed. However, an attorney who is skilled in the art of negotiating with insurance companies may (1) obtain a reduction in the amounts deducted from your settlement that will go to reimburse your first-party carrier, (2) arrange that your attorneys' fees are paid from the insurance company's share of the settlement, and (3) significantly increase the amount of money that you receive.

## Bill Submission and Payment

*If an insurance company requests that you see an Independent Medical Examiner, a doctor hired by them to dispute your claim, contact an attorney immediately. Under no circumstances should you attend an Independent Medical Exam without legal consultation!*

Under most automobile policies, payment for medical bills is based on the following factors:

- The treatment must be for injuries sustained as a result of the accident. Prior conditions are not allowed, although exacerbation or aggravation of prior medical conditions may be.

- The treatment must be necessary — that is, it is required to return you to the same condition you were in before the accident.

- The treatment charges must be reasonable. This means that the cost of the treatment is similar to what other care providers charge for the same service in the community.

An insurance company can reject claims for payment if any of the above criteria are not met to its satisfaction. If an insurance company rejects your claim for payment, you are not without recourse.

**If your care providers are denied payment, they are *not* entitled to sue your insurance carrier, because they do not have a contractual relationship with your insurance company. Your care providers can, however, sue *you* to collect outstanding amounts owed. If a claim dispute is not easily resolved, and your care providers are demanding payment, an attorney can be your professional negotiator. He or she can ensure payments to your care providers and, most importantly, protect you from damaging collection activity and potential lawsuits.**

First, review the insurance policy to determine if the rejection is unfounded. If you feel it is, ask your care providers to submit written support of your claims, with complete documentation.

Under insurance policy regulations, an insurance company must pay or deny a bill within 30 days of its receipt. You or your health care provider are obligated to provide the documentation. If you do not, the insurance company may reject the claim, or require you to see a doctor employed by them (an "Independent Medical Examiner") to validate your claims for care and make a determination of whether they should pay the claim.

If there is a dispute over payment, reread the insurance policy under which you have submitted your claim. Every policy contains language defining how disputes should be handled. Quite often, the policy stipulates that arbitration is the required method of dispute resolution. Other policies may require mediation, or a determination by the state court system.

## Summary

The first step in achieving full physical and financial recovery is a full review of all of the insurance options available to you. Once you know which insurance companies you're dealing with and who's going to pay for what, it's time to start documenting everything about your accident from A to Z. (And we'll get to *that* a little later in this book.)

Reviewing and understanding insurance policies may well be the most frustrating — and probably the most boring!— aspect of handling your own case. But it's something you've got to do early on if you hope to understand all of your options and opportunities for full settlement value. Making the time and taking the effort to investigate and clearly identify all of your insurance options means a much higher chance that you'll be able to successfully and fully recover from the losses caused by the automobile accident.

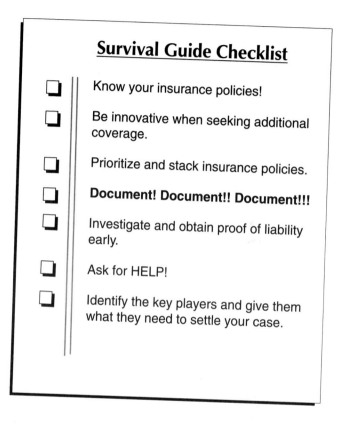

# Survival Guide Checklist

- ☐ Know your insurance policies!

- ☐ Be innovative when seeking additional coverage.

- ☐ Prioritize and stack insurance policies.

- ☐ **Document! Document!! Document!!!**

- ☐ Investigate and obtain proof of liability early.

- ☐ Ask for HELP!

- ☐ Identify the key players and give them what they need to settle your case.

# Graham Cracker

But Phil was unconcerned — he knew his PIP policy would cover it.

# Personal Injury Protection (PIP)

In Chapter 2 we reviewed some of the common insurance policies that you should investigate for potential reimbursement of your claims. Throughout your quest for insurance coverage, no stone should remain unturned. In this chapter, we'll go into greater detail about one of the most effective sources of immediate financial reimbursement in the event you're injured in an automobile accident. We're talking about "Personal Injury Protection," a type of insurance coverage that absolutely *nobody* should drive without.

## What is PIP?

Personal Injury Protection ("PIP") coverage is a limited contract between you and your insurance company that describes certain benefits you will receive if you are injured in an accident, *no matter who was at fault*. PIP benefits may include payment for lost wages, medical bills, loss of services, home nursing care, even death and funeral benefits. These bills can be paid by the insurance company as they are accrued. Surprisingly, this outstanding coverage is one of the least expensive options on an insurance policy. It costs you little to purchase, and if you have an accident and make a claim against your PIP policy, your insurance company must begin paying you right away.

## Why PIP?

*PIP coverage promotes maximum physical recovery.* It can protect you from the debilitating emotional trauma that can occur if you find yourself without adequate financial resources to protect you and your family from a sudden loss of income. Your physical recovery should be your top priority after an automobile accident. The faster you can get back on track financially, the better the chances that all of your energies — mental, emotional, and physical — can more quickly be directed to healing and recuperation.

*PIP coverage pays money to you regardless of who is at fault.* People often mistakenly assume that the at-fault driver's liability coverage provides all one needs to pay for medical and other costs incurred because of an automobile accident injury. However, liability coverage may be withheld by the insurance company if you are found to be at fault in the accident.

*PIP coverage is provided immediately following the accident.* The insurance company may delay payments under liability coverage until it receives all of the reports and records about your accident and injury and reviews them for a final determination of any reimbursements. This could take months (or even years in some disputed cases).

One of the most important features of standard PIP coverage is *payment for lost wages*. This is the insurance industry's version of "disability insurance." If you're injured so badly that you are unable to work, a $200-per-week cash benefit can very well be the difference between financial survival or disaster.

If you are injured on the job, the State of Washington Department of Labor and Industries may provide a percentage of your lost wages as soon as 14 days after you submit an Initial Injury Report. The report must state that you are unable to work because of the injury. Because *some claims take months to be accepted,* you may qualify for provisional payments while your claim is being evaluated. Your PIP benefits may be affected if you are also claiming L&I benefits.

What if you are injured in an accident, are unable to work and can't pay your *health* insurance premiums? This is one of the most important reasons why you should have PIP coverage. PIP will pay you lost wages and provide the income that you need to continue to pay your health insurance premiums. Your health insurance (e.g., Blue Cross) covers your necessary medical care while you are settling your claim with the third-party insurer. Under no circumstances should you allow your health insurance to lapse.

## How Much Does PIP Pay?

PIP policies pay at least $10,000 in medical bills per accident. **Washington State law now requires that all insurance companies offer a minimum of $10,000 of PIP coverage when they sell an automobile insurance policy.** So important is PIP coverage that if you decline to purchase it, you must do so in writing.

PIP coverage is included in *your* own automobile insurance. You can claim PIP benefits for you and your family when you're injured in an automobile accident while riding in your own or someone else's car. Any passengers who are injured in an automobile accident while riding in your car are also covered. PIP also covers you and your family as pedestrians.

An additional feature of PIP is that coverage is provided per accident. If you have more than one accident during the policy year, you may draw a total of $10,000 for the first accident, and an *additional* $10,000 for each accident during that year.

PIP policies can be purchased that provide up to $35,000 for medical for three years, and $35,000 wage loss for one year. You should talk to your insurance agent about PIP coverage options that go beyond the minimum standards required by law and may be beneficial to you and your family.

Beginning immediately after the accident, you may begin drawing on your PIP benefits to pay for hospital, Chiropractic, and certain out-of-pocket expenses. Most standard PIP policies pay 85% of your normal weekly wages, beginning on the fifteenth day following your accident. Your insurance carrier figures wage loss under your PIP coverage just like medical bills and out-of-pocket expenses. Once the maximum available amount covered by your PIP policy has been paid out, payments will stop.

**Minimum PIP coverage is good for three years from the date of the accident. Do not delay making a claim under your PIP coverage, or you may lose the opportunity to take advantage of this excellent coverage.**

Without PIP coverage, your medical and other related bills might remain unpaid until your case is settled. A year or more could go by before you see any money from the at-fault driver for lost wages, medical care, and the like. In the meantime, you are faced with the frustrations and fear of watching your savings dwindle, your credit suffer, or perhaps your mortgage being foreclosed because you have no income due to a disabling injury.

 Your automobile insurance policy may include "Med Pay" coverage. This type of coverage does *not* provide the protection of PIP. It is a medical-payments-only version of PIP, and doesn't cover wage loss or loss of services.

You may be unable to pay the medical bills that accumulate during your recovery after the accident. Past due bills can accrue finance charges that may not be reimbursed by the third-party insurer. It is not unusual at all to see thousands of dollars in medical bills following an automobile accident injury. Past due finance charges on these amounts can add up quickly. PIP coverage can provide the cash you need to make payments for your medical care before your case settles and avoid the additional expense of having to pay finance charges after settlement.

## PIP and Your Insurance Company

Your insurance company (the "first party carrier") will track the payments made under your PIP coverage. If your insurance company questions whether your medical treatment is reasonable and necessary, it may delay payment and request a records review or an Independent Medical Exam (IME). If the insurance company's doctor reports no objective findings of injury related to the accident, your PIP benefits may be terminated. Insurance companies want to keep their costs down, and they will terminate your benefits if you can't quickly document your injuries to their satisfaction.

**By law, your insurance premiums can't go up if you make a claim under your PIP coverage. Your PIP coverage exists to provide you with a ready source of funds to immediately pay your accident-related expenses. Use it or lose it!**

Be sure to follow your care provider's treatment plan to the letter, and submit all bills, expenses and records to the insurance company *immediately* so that you quickly receive reimbursement under your PIP coverage for these expenses.

Your care providers should send the bills and records for your treatment directly to your PIP carrier. The insurance company requires itemized bills and chart notes. They will carefully review them to confirm that all of the treatments are related to the accident. The insurance company may also request that your care providers provide additional records or detailed supplemental reports.

*Once you sign a settlement check offered by the third party insurance carrier, your PIP benefits provided by your first party insurance carrier stop. Make sure all of your financial losses are covered before accepting any settlement offer.*

If you or your care providers delay in providing bills or records to the insurance company, payments under your PIP coverage are likely to be delayed. If you are requesting reimbursement under PIP, you will need to carefully manage the distribution of appropriate information and communications between your insurance carrier and your medical team. This often requires follow-up phone calls or letters by you to confirm that requested information has been sent and received in a timely manner.

If you have more than one accident in a given year and are making claims on your PIP coverage for multiple accidents, the injuries received in each accident (and the respective costs incurred) must be segregated. The insurance company treats each incident separately. You must carefully document and keep separate the treatment and resulting costs that are incurred for each respective accident. This can become extremely complicated, especially if you receive similar or related injuries in more than one accident.

To understand how PIP payments for multiple accidents may be applied, consider this scenario. You are injured on March 1 in an automobile accident, and under your standard PIP coverage benefits you will be paid for that accident for three years following the date of the accident, to a maximum of $10,000.

Because this is going to be the worst year of your life, you are also injured in a second automobile collision on August 1 of that same year. Because PIP benefits are *per accident,* you can claim a maximum of $10,000 in benefits for the second accident for three years.

Let's say that the injuries that you received in the first accident on March 1 are successfully treated and you reach maximum medical improvement (MMI) seven months later on October 1. When you reach MMI, your PIP medical coverage stops. The payments under your PIP coverage for this first accident totalled $3,500.

Even if you continue to receive treatment for the injuries received in the *second* accident on October 1, you can't apply the "left over" benefits from the first accident to your treatment for the second accident. PIP benefits are paid per accident, and you can't combine treatment or benefits for multiple accidents.

If you are in an accident, your insurance agent may not volunteer that payments are available under your PIP coverage. Be sure to ask your agent about your PIP coverage. If it's available, don't hesitate to submit claims for payment under that coverage.

The insurance industry relies on an unspoken truth: the great majority of Americans simply don't want to fight the system. Don't allow your fear of duking it out with the insurance companies to keep *them* in the Billion Dollar Club and leave *you* without needed benefits or fair compensation for damage, loss, or injury. If you have PIP coverage, claim the benefits that are due to you.

Your insurance company may not be very aggressive about recommending that you accept the offer of PIP coverage now required by law. The money that your insurance company pays to you under your PIP coverage will be reimbursed later by the third party insurance company (the insurance company that provided coverage for the at-fault driver). However, between the time your insurance company pays you money under your PIP coverage and when they are reimbursed by a third party insurer, your insurance company is losing interest on that money.

*Because of the complexities of multiple accident injuries, these cases often fail to settle and end up in court. If you have been injured in more than one automobile accident, consider the advantages of retaining a personal injury attorney. He or she can assume the difficult task of managing your multiple claims and maximize your chances of achieving successful settlement without having to go to court.*

57

They in effect "take a loss" for the period of time before they are reimbursed.

If you don't have PIP coverage, or you're not certain if you do, call your insurance agent today and make sure this coverage is included in your policy. It's cheap protection!

Payments under PIP coverage will only be made if the PIP coverage was purchased and in effect *prior* to the accident for which you are claiming coverage.

## How Do I Claim My PIP Benefits?

Here is the checklist that provides all of the steps that you must complete in order to take full advantage of your PIP coverage and receive the benefits that you need while receiving treatment for your injuries.

### PIP Benefits Checklist

❏ Call your insurance agent to report the accident.

❏ Confirm that you have PIP or Med Pay.

❏ If yes, determine the time and dollar amount limits.

❏ Ask your agent to: (1) take your Report of Loss claim; (2) phone in your report to the claims office; and (3) call you back with the claim number, address, and phone number of the claims office.

❏ Call the claims office and get the name of the claims adjuster who is handling your claim. Ask the claims adjuster to mail a PIP Application, Attending Physician's Report, and Salary Verification forms.

❏ Complete the PIP Application and return it to the claims adjuster.

❏ Have your doctor fill out the Attending Physician's Report and return it to you. Mail it to the claims adjuster.

❏ Have your employer complete the Salary Verification form and return it to you. Mail it to the claims adjuster.

❏ Provide your claim number and the adjuster's name, office address, and phone number to all of your health care providers.

❏ Instruct your health care providers to bill your PIP carrier directly. Make sure they send chart notes with each billing statement.

❏ Continue to review and manage your health care to ensure efficient and timely receipt and payment on your claims for PIP benefits. Monitor all payments to make sure you aren't caught financially unprepared by the expiration of available benefits.

## Plan Ahead!

When your PIP benefits expire (either after reaching maximum payout or maximum time limit under the policy), this is an opportune time for the third party insurance carrier to increase the pressure on you to settle. They know that you may soon be experiencing a frightening financial crisis and will be more likely to settle too soon and for far less than full value.

The best way to avoid getting yourself in such a losing situation is to *plan ahead*. Manage your treatment plan and recovery with an eye to the future. Ask your medical team to outline anticipated treatment and related costs early in your treatment plan. Compare the anticipated costs and duration of treatment with all of the combined insurance benefits that are available to you.

If early on in your treatment you determine that there is a chance that your PIP and other insurance benefits may run out before you'll be able to return to work and regain your financial security, incorporate this knowledge in your settlement negotiation strategy. Be prepared to hold out for as long as your medical treatment requires. Avoid the pitfalls of settling too early for too little because of mounting financial pressures.

If you realize that the insurance benefits that you've identified so far will not adequately cover your financial needs while you are negotiating a settlement, consider professional assistance. A personal injury attorney can often identify alternate sources of insurance benefits that you never even considered and help you manage the complexities of obtaining benefits from multiple insurance policies. In addition, settlement negotiations conducted by an experienced professional will often result in quicker settlement with a higher financial value.

When you have PIP coverage, your insurance company takes the financial loss while you are negotiating a settlement with the third party insurance company. If you don't have PIP, *you* take the loss. When your insurance agent offers PIP coverage, don't think twice — *just do it!*

## Summary

The diligent consumer investing their insurance premium dollars year after year rarely gets a reasonable return on their investment in the insurance industry. Occasionally, however, changes occur in the industry that clearly benefit the consuming public. Personal Injury Protection coverage, now actively promoted by Washington State law, provides the consumer with a ready source of financial reimbursement during the time when it is often most desperately needed.

The substantial benefits available under even minimum PIP coverage often mean financial survival for automobile accident victims. Know your insurance policies and use your PIP coverage to protect you and your family against the threats to your financial security that are so often generated by automobile accident injury.

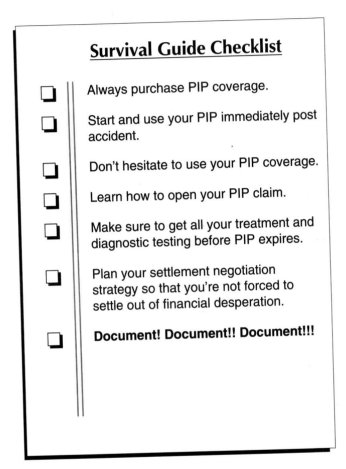

## Survival Guide Checklist

☐ Always purchase PIP coverage.

☐ Start and use your PIP immediately post accident.

☐ Don't hesitate to use your PIP coverage.

☐ Learn how to open your PIP claim.

☐ Make sure to get all your treatment and diagnostic testing before PIP expires.

☐ Plan your settlement negotiation strategy so that you're not forced to settle out of financial desperation.

☐ **Document! Document!! Document!!!**

# NOTES

# Handling Your Own Claim

Now we come to what this book is really all about: Handling your own insurance claim. If you've come this far, then we haven't lost you in the gruesome horrors of automobile repair or the relentless nightmares of reading and understanding insurance policies. Don't worry — it gets better! In this chapter, we're going to provide an opportunity for you to really take a good look at yourself and your resources and make an informed decision about whether or not you're a good candidate for handling, negotiating, and settling your own case.

We've consolidated many years of experienced counsel and advice in this chapter and throughout this book. We believe that many people can successfully negotiate their own settlement claim. But we also believe that self-representation may not be the wisest route for everyone. In an effort to prepare you for what lies ahead as you begin to negotiate your own settlement claim, we'd like to give you as much knowledge and expertise as can possibly be included in the limited confines of a consumer resource guidebook.

Anyone who is considering negotiating a settlement of their own claim should carefully read this chapter and decide, before taking the big plunge into self-representation, if that's the most effective route to take. If you decide it's not for you, don't panic and feel that you're somehow inadequate. *You're not alone.* There are plenty of personal injury professionals who can handle your case for you and relieve you of all the demands, responsibilities, and just plain *work* that self-representation demands.

## Should I Represent Myself?

The legal system today is renowned for its complexity, delays, and often overwhelming frustrations and confusion. Many people would try to convince you that you'd be a fool to jump right into settlement negotiations on your own, without the benefit of legal representation.

Once you've mustered the courage to represent yourself, you'll then have to commit a great deal of your time and energy to drive your claim through the many roadblocks, setbacks, and stalemates that are the standard operating procedure of the insurance trade. You will only be successful if you are able to maintain a psychological, physical, and spiritual balance throughout the settlement negotiations.

Many people, however, do just that. They manage to stay on top without sinking under the weighty demands of going up against the powerful insurance industry. And the ones who do make it on their own do so for three very distinct reasons: they have the **time**, the **temperament**, and the **talent**. You *must* have all three of these qualities, and in large doses, before you consider representing yourself.

## The Three Major Qualifiers

There are some very good reasons why you should represent yourself and settle your own insurance claim. Industry experts claim that a majority of all insurance settlements are made with people who represent themselves. We call these folks "pro se." Out of this vast group of people who have suffered some type of damage or injury, some even win close to the full value of their claim.

Others, however, don't. And it always boils down to the same three failures: they didn't have the time, the temperament or the talent to successfully represent themselves against the insurance machine.

Let's take a look at these characteristics. As you read the next sections, you are going to have to be very, very honest with yourself. Before you decide to represent yourself against an insurance company, you need to be absolutely certain that you possess all three personal characteristics. Because if you *don't* have these qualities, and you *do* decide to take on the insurance industry, you will most likely be soundly stomped. When all is said and done, if you tackle self-representation without adequate preparation and the required skills, you may find yourself in even worse physical and psychological condition after settlement than you were in before.

Do you need an attorney? To successfully negotiate your claim, or take your case to court and win, you need to answer with a resounding and confident "YES!" the following questions: "Do I have the *time?*" "Do I have the *temperament?*" and "Do I have the *talent?*" If you answer no to any of these key questions, you may be better served by competent legal counsel who has spent years developing settlement and litigation expertise.

Now is the time to examine your options, and make sure that you're in the best possible position when you take your claim to the insurance company.

## Time

One of the primary reasons that insurance companies make so much money and pay out so little is that they learned long ago that if they hassle, badger, torment, and just plain *pick on* the typical claimant hard enough, often enough, and long enough, the claimant will finally break down and give up the good fight. Claimants soon reach that inevitable point where they throw up their hands and say, *"That's it, I give up, I can't take this any more, just cut me the darn check!"* 'Tis the sweetest song ever heard by the insurance adjuster!

Insurance adjusters are professionally trained in tactics and strategies that are specifically designed to stretch out your claim and your financial resources, weaken your emotional reserves, and poke great gaping holes in your case. They blow you away and then they sweep you right into the corner of total surrender where, not too surprisingly, the adjuster is waiting for you with a settlement check in hand and a warm, understanding smile.

So how do you beat the insurance company at its own game? *By putting time on your side.* When you decide to represent yourself, you are making a large commitment of your free time — or freeing up time otherwise committed!— to many different tasks that are required if you are to successfully settle your case.

**Be A Telephone Junkie.** From the time of your accident to the time of settlement, you will need to make dozens, if not hundreds, of telephone calls. First to your insurance agent, and probably the other party's insurance agent. Then to the towing company, the storage yard, and the car rental agency. You'll also be calling the auto body shop and other collision repair specialty shops. Phone calls to health care providers requesting appointments, follow-up care, records, and billing information will also consume a large part of your settlement efforts. If your ability to remain employed is affected by the accident, you may also find yourself dealing on the telephone with your employer and other agencies that are involved in tracking and paying disability benefits.

**Medical Care Team.** If you are injured in the accident, there may be multiple care providers, such as a general practitioner, Chiropractor, neurologist, dentist, physical therapist or psychologist, to whom you will need to make telephone calls to arrange appointments, request tests, and obtain test results. Transferring test results, x-rays, and other medical documentation between the specialists handling your case must be carefully choreographed with upcoming appointments. Any time you make such a request, you should follow up with a confirming phone call to make sure your request was successfully handled. At each step in your medical care, you must notify the insurance companies handling the claim so that they can adjust their reserves accordingly and advise you of any coverage limitations.

**Eyewitness Accounts.** If there are witnesses to the accident, you will need to contact these individuals immediately and arrange for supporting documentation, written testimony, or reports. Such witnesses are often difficult to track after the accident, so it's very important that you contact them just as soon after the accident as possible, either by telephone, letter or personal visit.

**Documentation.** One of the most important tools in your arsenal against the insurance company is documentation. Photocopies, photographs, written and signed statements, diagrams, official documents and records, test results, and anything and everything that corroborates or supports your claim must be gathered and presented to the insurance company as you negotiate your claim.

**Communicating with Your Employer.** If the accident affects your ability to work, you must contact your employer regularly to advise them of your status and obtain the necessary sick leave, vacation time or unpaid leave during your recovery.

**Transportation.** Keeping medical appointments, meeting with the appraisers, making photocopies, meeting with eyewitnesses, retrieving and dropping off medical supplies, rotating your car with a rental car, dropping the kids off at child care while you attend appointments... it can be an exhausting itinerary of driving here, there, and seemingly everywhere to handle all the aspects of your claim. If your medical care is neither well-managed nor placed early on with the appropriate specialists, be prepared to spend entire days traveling from appointment to appointment.

**Daily Diary.** Track and document each telephone call, appointment, interview or conversation in a record book. Do *not* make the mistake of depending on your memory. This is especially important if you have been injured in the accident. Ten months down the line, the insurance company may demand ample and accurate documentation detailing all of the damages that you suffered because of the accident. Without accurate records, they may dispute your offhand recollection of what did or didn't happen during your recovery.

**Do I Have the Time?** We're talking about time here, and lots of it, probably several hours each day. If you are working full-time, or managing an active household, or actively participating in retirement activities, you may not be able to meet the additional demands on your time that are generated by self-representation.

If you were injured in the accident, you must remember that your physical recovery is of paramount importance. You must *not* rob from the time that has been set aside by your medical caregivers for rest, healing, and recovery. To do so may delay your recovery, inevitably increase your medical costs, and exhaust you physically, mentally, and emotionally.

If you were already pressed for time before the accident, think twice about committing time that you already *don't* have to pursue complex and demanding settlement negotiations that will demand many hours each week.

Most importantly, if you were injured in the accident, think *twice more* about the potential damage you will be doing to your body and your mind if you undertake the stressful and demanding activities of self-representation. *The damaging effects may be permanent, and no amount of settlement money will buy back your health and well-being.*

If you can honestly say that you do have the time to conduct all of the activities that are required to settle your own claim, congratulations! You have passed the first test. Many people have courageously gone before you and have successfully managed the many demands of dealing with insurance companies one-on-one. If you are able to *find* the time, you may find that *devoting* that time to the settlement cause may result in successful settlement of your claim.

## Temperament

What kind of person or personality wins a decent settlement from an insurance company?

A persistent person! Someone who doesn't give up easily and who is not easily intimidated by professionally trained tacticians. When we're talking "temperament," we mean those qualities in a person that make him or her a suitable candidate for enduring long periods of frustration, denial, and manipulation. The same qualities will compel the individual to take a personal stand and *not waver from it for one moment.*

"Stubbornness" may seem a likely component of the "right stuff" for handling your own case. Surprisingly, though, it's *flexibility* that will prove to be your ticket to surviving the insurance scrimmage. You simply can *not* let the tactics and strategies of the insurance company *get to you.* And remember that "getting to you" is *exactly* what the insurance adjuster is committed to doing.

You must be absolutely dogged in your determination to win. This does *not* mean that you should be abrasive, rude, hostile or dishonest. It *does* mean that you should be prepared to repeat your demands over and over and over again, and then just one more time for good measure, calmly, clearly, and precisely. When they say "no," you must have the enthusiastic desire to turn that into a "maybe" and the willful determination to make it a "yes."

A person with the right temperament simply does not just "go away." You believe in your case, and nothing the insurance company says, does, or *threatens* to do will dissuade you from your mission of a fair settlement. You must marshal all of the required documentation, testimony, and test results and use them *creatively* to support your case.

The facts are presented in a factual manner and so, too, are the emotional aspects of your claim. The people with the "right" temperament are not apologists. They are able to articulate and substantiate their complaints without feeling uncomfortable that others may think they are "whining." In a reasonable, logical, and adult manner, those individuals communicate their demands clearly and believe in the value of their claim.

**Changing Temperaments.** Temperament, of course, can change over time. We may begin our settlement negotiations coolly and calmly, and after a month or two of beating our heads against the Walls of Insurance, there may be a ragged edge to our voice and a peculiar gleam in our eye. Certainly, nobody is completely immune from the effects of taking repeated abuses from any quarter, least of all from an insurance company. But the person with a suitable temperament for self-representation must be able to endure all of the rigors and slide through the many hassles (both perceived and real) that go with the territory. Their aim is always on the goal of successful settlement.

One's natural temperament can also go through drastic changes after an injury. A slowly healing injury and the unremitting chronic pain it may cause can prevent even the most Herculean survivor from functioning as their former level-headed, good-natured, and rational self. Financial stresses, bill collectors, family tensions, inability to exercise, sudden weight gain, or the inability to perform on the job or even stay employed at all, can all have *disastrous* effects on one's physical, mental, and spiritual well-being.

If you have been injured in an accident, even your fabulously *sterling* personality can undergo changes that may adversely affect your ability to handle the stresses and demands of self-representation. Again, *your physical recovery is the most important thing following an injury accident.* You will need to put *all* of your personal resources into recovery after the accident. Committing even a fraction of those resources elsewhere may not be the smartest thing to do.

**Do I Have the Temperament?** While you may have been a perfect candidate for self-representation *before* the accident, think very carefully about your state of physical and mental health *now* before committing so much of yourself to what may be an extended period of settlement negotiations. Are you feeling stressed? Depressed? Angry? Are you experiencing pain, or are your abilities limited because of the accident? Are you dealing with family tensions, employment stresses, or financial difficulties? Any one of these situations can dramatically impact your ability to maintain the right frame of mind while you are pursuing your claim.

Remember that the typical insurance company has unlimited time, unlimited resources, and an unlimited desire to win. If your injuries make it doubtful that you can compete on their level, do yourself a favor: *don't even try.*

If you're convinced that you've got the time and the temperament, you've almost got the winning combination to settle your own case! Let's take a look at the last and probably most important attribute: talent. Everybody has some — but let's see if yours is the *right* kind.

## Talent

When talking about "talent," let's focus on the skills and abilities that dictate the difference between success and failure in settlement negotiations. Just about everyone thinks of themselves as a decent negotiator. You get a good deal here, a great buy there. The truth is, however, that truly good negotiation skills *don't come naturally.* They're learned, developed, and honed to precision only after years of experience marked by some failures and many successes.

This is where the average lay person and the insurance company are most at odds. The insurance company is dedicated to two things: One, obtaining *control* of the situation. And two, *maintaining* that control. They are able to do this because they are excellent negotiators and skilled tacticians. They know the claims business inside and out. It's not often that the average person has the same scope and depth of negotiating experience.

If you are unable to grab control of your claim straight out of the gate, it is highly unlikely you will ever be able to wrestle it from the insurance company somewhere down the line. Once lost, it's almost impossible to regain control during the settlement negotiations.

Typically, an insurance company will assign an adjuster to close your claim in 48 hours. If that is not accomplished, your case may be assigned to another adjuster, who specializes in closing claims in five days or less. If on the fifth day your case isn't closed, yet *another* adjuster steps in. He is assigned the responsibility of closing your case in two weeks. After him comes the next adjuster, who is the one-month specialist. And so on. Each of these individuals will use professional, practiced sales techniques on the unsuspecting consumer. They know all the angles. They know exactly what to say to convince and sometimes badger the claimant to sign on the dotted line and close the claim.

**Do I Have the Talent?** We cannot within the limited scope of this book teach you the negotiating skills that you need to survive and win against the insurance giants. However, if you have *professional* training or experience in negotiating, including setting strategies and planning specific tactics, you may well possess the third and most crucial skill, the talent for negotiating, that will ensure successful self-representation.

If you do not have this kind of experience under your belt and cannot use it when the going gets hot and heavy, you may lose some extremely important bargaining points in the process. Once this happens, you're likely to end up watching helplessly as the settlement amount of your claim suffers.

We've covered the three major attributes of the winning settlement claimant: **time**, **temperament,** and **talent**. If this successful combination describes you, then congratulations! You're a natural winner! You'll most likely prevail against the insurance company. Put everything you've got into your case, stay focused, remain truthful, don't be dissuaded by threats and stalling techniques, and document, document, document! Take it to the wall and *win*!

## How Does the "System" Treat Pro Se Claimants?

So you've decided to represent yourself. Welcome to the community of competent people like you who have the abilities to state their case and stick to their guns. There are some things you should know and apply as you begin your journey down the road of self-representation.

**Medical Providers**. You must be very diligent throughout your medical care! Medical specialists do not often communicate with specialists in other fields. For example, unless you *proactively* manage your medical care, your Chiropractor may not know what your neurologist has already diagnosed. This may lead to lapses in treatment that will prove to be damaging to your health, and may increase your medical costs as well. *You* must assume the responsibility of making sure that all the important information is shared among your medical providers. If one specialist asks for test results from another, it's up to you to make sure the results get delivered.

If you are experiencing symptoms or problems following the accident, you must be especially consistent about communicating everything to your medical providers. While your dentist may not be very interested in the numbness in your hands, your neurologist most certainly will. Be aware of the various specialties. Volunteer all of the relevant information to the appropriate medical provider, and seek additional medical care from an alternative source if the situation demands it.

**Insurance Carriers**. As discussed in Chapter 2, you must be especially attentive to the various policies and coverage provided by all of the insurance carriers that are parties to your claim.

Insurance companies are less likely to take seriously those injured persons who represent themselves. Insurance professionals know that exerting the negotiating strategies of getting and maintaining control will more likely be effective against the average guy on the street than against an attorney.

**Just because you have chosen to appear pro se does *not* mean you receive *special* considerations. It only means that you receive the *same* considerations as the legal professionals who have studied and practiced the law for many years. You must be prepared to know and meet all of the legal require-ments if you choose to represent yourself. *Ignorance* is no excuse. This applies both during the settlement negotiation phase and during any courtroom litigation, should your case reach that point.**

Insurance companies have large financial reserves with which they can retain professional legal counsel. As a pro se claimant, you will be up against some very experienced litigators. The insurance companies hire attorneys who specialize in fighting legal issues in court. They are adept at persuading the jury and presenting the facts in the light that is least favorable to you. The jury may like you, and they may even believe you, but in the hands of a skilled courtroom tactician, your side of the case may be quickly clouded if not entirely forgotten by the time the defense attorney is finished presenting the insurance company's side of your case.

**Judges and Court Personnel**. The legal code of ethics demands that attorneys and others in the legal profession give the same, or greater, consideration and respect to individuals who are representing themselves. However, the legal code, Latin and all, also applies to *you* when you represent yourself.

While there are some instances in American folklore where the "underdog" is looked upon kindly by the judge and jury, in today's legal system this simply doesn't happen. The courts are stretched beyond capacity, and there are extraordinarily specific rules, regulations, and deadlines that *must* be followed to the letter. For example, if you miss a deadline to submit a brief (a type of legal document) to the court, the judge may not read it at all, and it may mean you lose your case.

Your complete preparation (including comprehensive documentation), well-groomed, professional appearance, and attention to every detail will send the message that you are to be taken seriously. An articulate, persuasive, consistent, and honest approach to all aspects of your case will lend additional credibility to your claim. Together, all of these things create the winning combination that produces a successful settlement.

But what should you do if you have honestly and diligently assessed your abilities and limitations and have discovered that you may not have what it takes to successfully settle your own claim?

## When Do I Need an Attorney?

Just as there are many reasons to settle your own insurance claim, there are also some compelling reasons why you should *not*. We've talked about time, temperament, and talent, and how important they are to your successful claim.

It needs to be said: there are certain cases that simply must be handled by a competent personal injury professional. If you have been representing yourself up to this point, and you suspect that now you may need an attorney, it may *not* be too late to hire an attorney to assume your case and pursue the highest value for your claim.

The first step is to select an attorney and call him or her and briefly outline your case on the telephone. Ask for an initial consultation. *Confirm that the initial consultation is free. If it is not, consider another attorney.*

The experienced personal injury attorney will meet with you and discuss the details of your case. Often, the attorney will advise you that there is no need for you to obtain legal counsel. The attorney should be able to provide some basic guidance during the consultation that will help you continue to successfully manage your own claim.

Sometimes, the attorney will evaluate your case and determine that it is too late for legal representation to have a significant impact on your case. Perhaps you already released information to the insurance company already that has irreparably compromised your case. Maybe you neglected to use certain insurance benefits before they expired.

Additionally, you may have already arrived at a settlement amount that cannot be raised significantly by the intervention of an attorney. In this situation, a competent attorney will advise you to take the offered settlement now, without legal representation. An attorney coming into the picture so late in the game may not increase the settlement value, and may actually *decrease* it because of attorney's fees.

However, certain situations following an automobile accident may require that you hire an attorney. Following are some warning signs that may indicate it's time for you to call a personal injury attorney *now*.

**If You Were Injured in the Accident**. Even a seemingly minor injury or discomfort can turn into a major medical expense later on, and may seriously affect your ability to work. If you have any suspicion that you were injured in the accident, you need the support of a legal professional who is experienced in assessing the claim value of your injury and managing your medical care, billing, and continued insurance coverage.

**If You Have No Insurance.** Many people mistakenly think that if they have no insurance, an attorney won't handle their case. Wrong! If you don't have first-party coverage (your own insurance policy), you won't have the advantage of having an insurance professional represent your insured losses. You need someone in your corner to protect you from the devastating physical and financial losses that can occur. If you don't have insurance of your own, it's easy to think that you're up the proverbial creek when it comes to getting monetary reimbursement from an insurance policy. But an attorney can step in immediately to represent you and deal directly with the at-fault driver's insurance company to protect your interests.

**If the Other Driver Has No Insurance.** It is very difficult tracking down the financial assets and recoverable funds of an uninsured driver. An attorney is more experienced than you in ferreting out the potential resources and possible alternative insurance policies (see Chapter 2) that may provide compensation for your injuries and losses.

**When the Insurance Company Asks for a Recorded Statement About the Accident.** Insurance companies are prepared to ask you leading questions that may elicit responses that may not be to your advantage when it comes time to settle. Especially in situations where fault is questionable, your statements may persuade an insurance company to place blame for the accident on you and thus diminish the value of your claim.

Anticipate that the insurance company will ask for a statement, and prepare a written statement ahead of time. Your "script" should contain the basic facts of the accident, a concise narrative of your injuries, and a chronological history of the medical care that you received as a result of the accident.

You would be amazed at how a simple response, such as *"Oh, I'm doing OK"* can sound in court like you were perfectly all right after the accident and suffered no injuries whatsoever. Your statements may be interpreted later as enthusiastic affirmations that you suffered no damages as a result of the accident, thus significantly reducing the value of your claim.

**When the Insurance Company Asks You to Sign an Authorization to Release Medical Records**. The insurance company will try to convince you that you must sign an authorization. Your own insurance company may tell you that if you don't sign the authorization, you are breaking the terms of the contract and they will drop your coverage. The truth is, you do not have to sign a blanket authorization for *all* medical records. *Never do this!* This allows an insurance company unlimited access to your old medical records, some of which may negatively affect your case. (How about that psychotherapy in 1976? Or the in-patient treatment for alcoholism in 1983?)

Rather, you should authorize release of only those medical records that apply *directly* to the accident. That is, between the date of the accident and the date the authorization is signed.

*It is not always easy signing a limited authorization for the insurance company. This is one situation where you may need the assistance of an attorney.*

**If You are Having Difficulties with Your Own Insurance Company**. If your own insurance company is stalling or otherwise giving you problems, this is *not* a sign of good things to come! Remember: you paid those insurance premiums for contracted coverage in the event you had an accident. While an insurance company may be slow to respond to an individual claimant, they are surprisingly responsive when an attorney picks up the phone and gives them a friendly jingle.

**If Your Insurance Company Requests an Independent Medical Examination**. If your insurance company requests that you see one of their contracted independent medical examiners, *do not under any circumstances agree to go without first obtaining legal consultation*. The doctor hired by your own insurance company may likely testify *against* you, because the doctor is hired by the insurance company to reduce the amount of money that the insurance company may have to pay on your claim. Remember, insurance companies are in the business to make a profit.

**If the Other Driver's Insurance Company is Out of State**. This is a red flag that often means you will be dealing with a substandard insurance company that may be operating under laws different from those in the State of Washington. Typically, you will be faced with extensive written correspondence and lengthy long-distance calls when attempting to communicate with these companies. The old adage, *"Out of sight, out of mind,"* applies all too frequently in these situations. If you are unable to deal in person with your adversary, your negotiations will suffer.

**If the Accident Caused a Minimal Amount of Property Damage.** The lower the property claim, the bigger the problem. Sounds odd, doesn't it? There's a simple reason for this warning: the insurance industry is extremely vigilant when it comes to fraud. When someone files a claim for injuries, and the damage to the automobiles involved is either minimal or non-existent, the insurance company begins to wonder how your claimed injuries could have happened when property damage was so minimal. A big red flag goes up in the adjuster's office and comes right back down onto the cover of your file: FRAUD!

*Insurance companies have special investigative units that are highly funded and specifically focused on identifying and prosecuting insurance fraud.*

Sometimes an innocent plaintiff gets involved in fraud investigations because they unknowingly go to a medical practitioner who has already been targeted for fraudulent medical practices. If your case ends up being investigated for fraud, you will have quite a battle on your hands trying to convince the insurance company that your case is legitimate. You absolutely *must* have an attorney to help direct your claim away from the fraud division and back into the claims mainstream where it will be evaluated fairly and settled reasonably.

**If You Had a Pre-existing Medical Condition.** Insurance companies love to jump on the "pre-existing bandwagon." They will insist that any injuries you are claiming now are, in fact, old injuries that you've had forever. If they get their hands on old medical records that document a pre-existing condition, you may have a tough time compelling the insurance company to ante up any money for medical treatment or other damages.

An experienced attorney will know how to present your injuries in the accident separate and apart from any other pre-existing conditions. Also, an accomplished legal professional can implement the "egg shell" theory. This in essence says that if you hit someone who already has a very fragile skull and crack their head, you have committed no less a serious injury to that person than if you'd hit someone with a head like Hulk Hogan. The person with the fragile head is hurt even *worse* than the healthy person, and the at-fault party is responsible for the more serious injuries.

Contrary to what the insurance industry would like us all to believe, people with pre-existing conditions do *not* cruise the highways and slam their brakes in search of convenient ways to exacerbate their injuries and relive the pain and disability they suffered in an earlier accident!

**If You're Just Not the Same Old You**. Last, but far from least, we include the final indicator of when you should hire an attorney. We call this the "On the Edge" test.

Have you lost your sense of humor? Are you depressed because you can't work or play like you used to before the accident? Does every little thing take you to your wit's end? Do you feel like everything is piling up and you can't see your way out from under the mounting stress? Do you feel like you're living in some strange and scary place where NOTHING is going right? Then you need an attorney to help alleviate the stress of an accident injury before it destroys the quality of your life now and in the future.

## How Can an Attorney Help Me?

If you decide to hire an attorney, you'll want to read Chapter 5. That chapter goes into much greater detail about finding an attorney and working with him or her throughout your personal injury case.

For purposes of this chapter, let's review some of the basic ways that an attorney can help you to determine the highest claim value for your case, obtain the best settlement, and return you to your pre-accident physical, mental, and emotional state of health.

**Controlling the Case**. A qualified personal injury attorney can literally take control of your case and dictate the timing, manner, tone, and substance of the case. This is exactly what the insurance company will do to *you* if you are not adequately represented, either by yourself or by an attorney. With competant representation, the tables are turned. Negotiations cease to be so one-sided in the insurance company's favor.

**Managing the Care Providers**. Your attorney acts as the "executive" who oversees all aspects of your medical care. Because medical specialists don't often communicate across the lines of their own specialties, an attorney can provide the communication and coordination between different practitioners. This can mean the difference between inadequate or inappropriate care, and comprehensive, pro-active, and complete care. Also, many times a patient simply can't, or forgets to, communicate important things about what is going on with their bodies or their minds after an accident.

The patient may be physically or emotionally unable to manage all of the demands presented by multiple care providers. This is especially true if the patient is seriously injured, or has suffered a head injury that limits their ability to think clearly or function at 100% capacity.

**Managing medical and other bills**. The typical injury-causing automobile accident generates voluminous forms, authorizations, records, statements, and bills. There must be received, appropriately processed, and filed in a timely manner. A skilled attorney and his or her support staff will gladly undertake the management of the "paperwork mountain" as part of your overall case. Most people cave in to insurance demands for early and inadequate settlement because they simply can't manage the day-to-day paperwork generated by a typical settlement claim.

If insurance billings are delayed or improperly paid, the medical providers are not paid promptly and they inevitably put pressure on the patient. This is the last thing you need if you are already dealing with the other stresses caused by the accident! Turning all of this over to your attorney means peace for your mind, and a stress-free healing and recovery time for your body.

**Persuading the Insurance Company**. A legal professional skilled in personal injury cases is experienced in the art of negotiation and persuasion. With the added support of extensive law office personnel, an attorney can present a very professional and effective case to the insurance company. Professionally written correspondence, effective graphical documentation, descriptive videotapes, compelling witness interviews, and effective management of independent medical examinations are the strengths of a winning settlement claim. These highly effective negotiating tools are "second nature" to an experienced personal injury lawyer.

**Fearlessly Advocating for the Client**. An attorney who specializes in personal injury has many years of experience working with injured plaintiffs, insurance companies, medical providers, employers, and all the other parties that are drawn into the vortex of your automobile accident, injury, and recovery.

It's "heads up!" time if you are facing physical pain and recovery, emotional trauma, or family stresses, or if your economic livelihood is threatened or ended altogether, or if you can no longer enjoy the pleasures that before the accident brought the good things your way. It may seem like everything that could possibly go wrong is coming down on you when you can least handle it on your own.

Your attorney can speak for you and act on your behalf, insulating you from the additional traumas and stresses caused by everyone wanting something from you that you simply are unable to give while you are recovering from your accident.

Once you have established a trusting, open, and co-operative relationship with your attorney, he or she will prove to be your "best friend" throughout the ups and downs of your recovery and settlement process. A good personal injury attorney is comforting, reassuring, and supportive, yet is able to deal aggressively and convincingly with the insurance companies.

Actually, multi-tasking is what a personal injury attorney does *second* best. What your attorney will do best of all is look out for your best interests and maximum settlement value during all phases of your settlement negotiations.

## Summary

In our personal injury practice, we talk and meet every day with people who have tried to settle their own insurance claim and for one reason or another have become convinced that they're stuck, they just can't do it any more, and they want us to step in and take over. We review their claim with them and talk a little bit about how they've been conducting their negotiations with the insurance company.

Of course, we do meet some folks who are truly stuck, either because theirs is a very complex case or they simply are physically or emotionally unable to handle the demands of self-representation.

But you'd be surprised how often we're able to quickly identify just what is needed to improve their strategy and produce a successful settlement. With a few words to the wise and some helpful, supportive guidance, we're able to put many people back on track and send them on their way to their *own* successful claim settlement, without professional legal representation.

If after reading this chapter you decide that you are a good candidate for negotiating your own settlement claim, then we've succeeded in doing what we set out to do when we wrote this book. You're likely feeling ready and enthusiastic about reading the rest of this guide, developing your most effective strategies, and negotiating the highest possible value for your claim. Perhaps most surprising of all, you'll have fun doing it!

## Survival Guide Checklist

☐ First, assess whether you have the time, temperment, and talent for self-representation.

☐ Look before you leap — self representation isn't for everyone.

☐ If you do decide to represent yourself, be prepared.

☐ Write out a statement on how the accident occurred, your injuries, treatment, and wage loss, and stick to it.

☐ Quick settlements are rare; prepare to negotiate.

☐ **Document! Document! Document!!**

☐ Keep your sense of humor, and be **persistent**.

☐ Nobody said it was easy, but you *can* do it, and win!

☐ Know when to ask for help.

☐ Know the warning signs that earmark your case for negotiation difficulties.

**NOTES**

# Finding the Right Attorney

In Chapter 4, you learned how to determine if you should handle your case on your own or obtain the help of a qualified personal injury attorney. In this chapter, you'll find out how to find a personal injury attorney. You'll also learn how to determine if that attorney is *qualified* to handle your personal injury case. We'll also cover some of the typical fees and costs of personal injury representation and identify the arrangements that provide the maximum financial benefit for you.

## What is a Personal Injury Attorney?

There are many different "specialties" in the field of law. Some attorneys limit their practice to tax cases; others specialize in business law, and there are a great number who specialize in family law, which includes divorce, child custody, and the like.

A great number of attorneys, however, don't really specialize in a particular area. Just like the many doctors who provide comprehensive, general care to their patients, we call these attorneys "general practitioners." They provide a much-needed source of legal expertise and advice to their clients for wide-ranging legal matters.

You may have worked with an attorney who provided great legal advice on that real estate deal in '88. It may well be that the family law attorney who handled your divorce is a terrific lady and a real go-getter in the courtroom. But if you have been involved in an automobile accident, especially one in which you have been injured, it's important to consult with an attorney who has many years of focused experience in the field of law that deals with automobile accident litigation. These attorneys are specialists in personal injury, or "PI" for short.

TRAFFIC ADVISORY TUNE TO 800 422-4610

*If you have been injured in an automobile accident, and even if you have already decided to settle your case on your own, schedule a consultation with an experienced personal injury attorney. During the initial interview, an experienced PI attorney will review your case and provide basic guidance free of charge.*

## Finding a Good Referral

There are a few tried-and-true ways to find a good personal injury attorney. There are also some pitfalls to avoid.

The most effective way to find a good, reputable personal injury attorney is to ask people you know and trust. Family, friends, and business associates may have personal experiences working with a personal injury attorney. Your employer may be able to recommend a personal injury attorney with whom your company has had contact on behalf of an injured employee.

When you ask trusted family members or friends to recommend a personal injury attorney, *get curious*! Ask them about their personal experience with the attorney. A few of the questions you may want to ask are:

## Attorney Referral Checklist

❏ Did the attorney keep promises to call back and take appropriate action?

❏ Was the attorney professional, efficient, and readily available?

❏ Did the attorney regularly communicate with the client, providing informative phone calls, letters, reports, and the like?

❏ Did the settlement proceed smoothly and in a timely manner, or did it seem to drag on and on without any resolution in sight?

❏ Did the case go to trial, and if so, did the original attorney handle the trial litigation?

❏ Did the attorney win a satisfactory settlement or a good outcome at trial?

❏ Were the attorney's fees and costs reasonable?

❏ Was the injured person satisfied with the experience and happy with the outcome?

❏ Would the injured person go back to that same attorney to handle another personal injury claim? If not, why not?

In addition to family and friends, another excellent source of good referrals is your medical practitioner. If you have been injured in an automobile accident and want to talk to an attorney about your case, ask your medical caregiver to recommend an attorney. Most likely, your doctor has had experience working with personal injury attorneys and can recommend a good one.

Places to *avoid* when seeking a referral to a personal injury attorney are television and radio advertisements. Many of these commercials are produced out-of-state and offered "cooperatively" to attorneys throughout the country. Such advertisements may indicate that a particular attorney is experienced in personal injury. As you will quickly learn, more than limited experience is required to qualify an attorney to successfully settle your claim.

Remember that your medical caregivers and your attorney will work together with you as a team to negotiate a successful settlement. If your doctor has already experienced professional, courteous, and competent contact with a personal injury attorney, she will be happy to share that referral with you, and you will become part of an established, successful team.

Many attorneys now advertise in the Yellow Pages of local telephone directories. This is a good place to find an attorney who is conveniently located near your home or business. However, under Washington law, attorneys may not advertise that they specialize in a particular area of law, such as personal injury.

## Your First Phone Call

Your first point of contact with a prospective personal injury attorney is likely to be a telephone call to his or her office. This first contact is very important. The following checklist will help you to decide at that point if it's worth your while to visit the attorney for an in-person evaluation of your case.

- Was your telephone call answered promptly, without a busy signal, prolonged hold or diversion to voice mail?

- Was the receptionist courteous, professional, and willing to direct your call promptly to the appropriate attorney or paralegal?

- Did the attorney or paralegal to whom you spoke give you their undivided attention on the phone?

- Did the attorney or paralegal clearly and without hesitation provide a satisfactory rundown of the attorney's qualifications for handling personal injury cases?

- Did the attorney or paralegal ask you specific questions about your case? For example:

  1. What was the date of the accident?

  2. Were you injured?

  3. What medical care have you obtained?

    4. Do you require additional medical care?

    5. What insurance is available?

- Did the attorney or paralegal offer to set an appointment for you to come in and discuss your case, free of charge, to obtain the necessary information to fully evaluate your case?

If you can answer "yes" to all of the above questions, then you are probably on the right track toward finding a qualified personal injury attorney.

## Warning Signs!

Warning signs that you are on the *wrong* track include:

- An office staff that is not enthusiastic or helpful, or seems inconvenienced by your call.

- You find it frustrating or impossible to get to a "live person," or your phone calls go unreturned.

- Once you are put in touch with an attorney or paralegal, they do not give you their undivided attention (put you on hold, carry on side conversations, continue to munch that extraordinarily *crisp* green salad....).

- The attorney or paralegal waits for *you* to ask all the questions, without initiating a thorough, preliminary screening of the facts of your case.

- Straight off the bat, the attorney or paralegal suggests a high dollar value to your case and makes promises of getting a fast cash settlement for you. *This is a significant warning sign that you are not dealing with a professional operation!*

## The Initial Consultation

If the attorney passes your first telephone contact with flying colors, you can now proceed to the next step: the free initial consultation, probably held in the attorney's office. This provides you with a second and more effective opportunity to assess first-hand the attorney's qualifications and ability to be your best representative.

When you arrive at the initial consultation, ask yourself the following questions:

*Is the main office area clean, organized, and professional appearing?* Personal injury cases require tremendous amounts of paperwork, forms, reports, and the like. A disorganized office means disorganized files. When you have deadlines to meet and legal papers to file on time, you don't want your attorney wasting precious time trying to track down lost paperwork in a cluttered office.

*Were you greeted professionally by a designated staff person upon your arrival?* The receptionist is the first point of contact for most businesses. Consequently, a professional business will put great

*If you are invited to an initial consultation and informed that you will be billed an hourly charge, decline the invitation and continue your search. Any personal injury attorney worth his or her salt will provide the first consultation free of charge, and advise you during that consultation whether or not you need an attorney to handle your case. It's free advice, and it's <u>good</u> advice!*

effort into hiring personable, professional front office staff. If the receptionist is unprofessional, disinterested, or discourteous, you know right away that this is an office that doesn't care about how it treats its clients, and it won't care about how it treats your case, either.

*Were you made to wait beyond your designated appointment time in a crowded waiting area?* If you've been asked to wait a few minutes for your appointment, there is probably no reason to worry. However, if you've been sitting more than a few minutes and nobody bothers to give you an update on your appointment time, be wary. If there are others like you in the waiting area who are inconvenienced by a delay in their scheduled appointment time, this is a sign of a poorly run office that has little regard for the comfort and convenience of clients.

*Do the office staff appear professional? Do they seem enthusiastic and positive about their jobs?* These people are the folks who will be handling many of the day-to-day, administrative activities of your case. A law office that cares about the well-being and satisfaction of its employees will automatically apply that same concern to its clients.

## Assessing the Initial Interview

Once you have been introduced to the paralegal or attorney who is conducting the interview, you have the next and last opportunity to assess the attorney's qualifications to handle your case.

Some preliminary questions that you should ask your-self are:

*Were you adequately introduced to the attorney handling the interview? Did the attorney greet you by name?* If not, then you may be speaking with someone who does not put a great deal of effort into even the most basic details. During settlement of a personal injury case, details matter.

---

In Washington state, many law firms now em-ploy paralegals to perform legal activities that were previously performed only by attorneys. Qualified paralegals have years of advanced training plus several years of professional law office experience. If you are interviewed by a paralegal rather than an attorney, evaluate the paralegal's professional demeanor just as you would an attorney's. After all, a paralegal works closely with the attorney and will likely reflect the attorney's own professionalism.

---

*Is the office used for the interview comfortable, neatly organized, and private?* First impressions are lasting ones. If you're uncomfortable during the interview, figure out why, and take note that your discomfort may continue through the dura-tion of your relationship with this particular attorney.

*Is the attorney familiar with the facts of your case that you had provided over the telephone?* If you have to repeat everything, then you are encounter-ing either a breakdown in communications or

If the staff appear unmotivated, blase or just downright unhappy, move on to another attorney and a working environment that says "We are winners!" in both words **and** actions.

inattention to detail — both are warning signs of things to come.

*Did the attorney provide a quick background of his or her qualifications and the history of the law practice?* Professional pride in accomplishments and expertise should be evident. The attorney should gladly share with you some background on his or her own practice and the practice of the law firm as a whole. Most lawyers will be able to provide you with a firm brochure or other publication that explains their area of practice and provides some historical background. If the attorney does not offer this information, ask the important questions listed in the Qualification Checklist below and form your opinion based on their responses.

*Does the attorney voluntarily explain to you what you can expect?* The anticipated time frame for settling your case, the attorney's anticipated activities and responsibilities, and your responsibilities should be clearly spelled out. The attorney should have a good feel for the work that your case will entail, and should voluntarily provide that information to you.

## That Old Familiar Feeling

It sounds silly, but it's true: *trust your gut instinct.* If during the initial meeting you like what you see and hear, do a quick "internal" check and ask yourself how you feel about the person on the other side of the desk.

Is she well-groomed? Friendly? Does she communicate well? Is she obviously interested in what you have to say, or is she more concerned with telling you what *she* wants to say? Most important: *do you like this person?*

Remember that you will be spending a great deal of time working closely with your attorney. He or she will represent you to the insurance companies and perhaps to a judge and jury. Do you feel comfortable when you imagine this person speaking on your behalf? Does the attorney instill a sense of confidence, and make you feel good about winning your case?

*You should be wary of the attorney who offers a quick dollar amount value to your case **before** reviewing the facts. A competent personal injury attorney will carefully evaluate all of the aspects of your case and provide a general value that will form the guidelines for negotiation with the insurance company.*

A successful settlement depends on successful communication between you and your attorney. If your *early* communications with an attorney don't feel "right," the *later* ones won't be a cakewalk, either!

During the initial interview, an attorney should do everything possible to put her best foot forward. If the attorney doesn't answer your questions to your satisfaction, or treats you with anything less than professional courtesy and respect, read the signals and realize that's probably as good as it's ever going to get — *and walk.*

**You pay an attorney to work <u>for</u> you. You have a right to demand excellence. If you don't get it up front, you won't get it later when it *really* counts.**

## Qualifying a Professional Injury Attorney to Handle Your Case

How can you tell if an attorney who offers to handle your case is "qualified?" There are a few things that you can ask an attorney during your first meeting that will let you quickly determine whether she is truly qualified to handle your case.

Many people hesitate to ask professionals about their qualifications. Some folks fear that they may appear rude or even "nosy" if they ask qualifying questions. If you're still thinking along these lines, *stop it!* You need to know if an attorney can handle and respond efficiently to the many complex demands of a personal injury case. An attorney in general practice, or one who specializes in real estate or family law, may be an outstanding legal professional, but he probably is *not* the best qualified attorney to handle your personal injury case.

Think of it this way: if you needed your tonsils removed, would you go to a foot doctor?

## When You Meet With an Attorney

Use the "**Qualification Checklist**" below as your evaluation bible when you are seeking a personal injury attorney. Don't hesitate to ask an attorney about his qualifications. A good attorney will welcome the opportunity to discuss his qualifications and review his personal injury experience with you.

On the other hand, an attorney who is probably not well-prepared to handle the complexities of a personal injury case may tend to avoid your questions, answer them in a vague or misleading way, or worst of all, defensively dismiss them altogether. Not a good sign!

If you have been injured in an automobile accident, you need to form a winning partnership with an attorney who will be working closely with you for months or even years. It's your responsibility, and your *right*, to make sure that the attorney you select to represent you has the education, experience, and ability to represent you professionally, diligently, and *successfully*. And only a qualified personal injury attorney will do.

To find out if an attorney is qualified to handle your case, ask the following questions:

## Attorney Qualifications Checklist

❏ *Where did you receive your law degree?* You may not know a law school from a beauty school, but this is a good question to gauge the response of the attorney. An attorney who is proud of his academic achievements at Little Wahoo U will show that in his response. Pride in accomplishments means pride in winning. A good sign!

❏ *Did you work in any other field before entering the field of law?* This provides you with an opportunity to find out a little bit about the background of the attorney. She may have spent five years working in the insurance industry and has a solid

109

familiarity with the insurance business. All to your benefit!

❑ *How long have you been practicing law?* Yes, every attorney needs that first big case to cut his milk teeth. But it doesn't have to be *your* case! Experience counts in the area of personal injury. An attorney who has years of experience dealing with many different insurance companies and who is well-versed in personal injury laws is going to provide the legal representation you need to successfully settle your case.

❑ *How long have you practiced law in the State of Washington?* Personal injury laws vary from state to state. An attorney who has just established a personal injury practice in the State of Washington may not be up to speed on the intricacies of the law in our state. Her lack of experience in this state may affect your ability to gain a good settlement.

❑ *Do you specialize in certain areas of the law? Do you regularly handle personal injury cases? What percentage of your practice is devoted to personal injury?* Your best bet is finding a personal injury attorney who devotes 100% of their practice to personal injury. Anything less than 80-90% means you may not be getting the professional experience and expertise that you need to successfully settle your case.

❏ *How much trial experience do you have?* It's important to remember that your case may not settle before it goes to court. You need to have a personal injury attorney who is capable of managing the many facets of insurance company negotiation and settlement, *plus* the completely different set of demands and responsibilities of courtroom litigation.

❏ *To which professional associations do you belong?* Organizational affiliations, such as the Trial Lawyers Association, indicate a professional who is dedicated to the law and committed to continued training and professional development.

❏ *How long have you been with this firm? With other firms?* An attorney who has moved from firm to firm may be very successful and on a fast track to bigger and better things. In the alternative, he may have been shuffled from one place to another because of poor performance or other professional difficulties. If there's a history of movement from firm to firm, ask why, and listen carefully to the response.

❏ *How many offices does this firm have?* A convenient location at which you can meet with your attorney is important, especially if you have been injured and face transportation difficulties.

❏ *What are your hours?* If the office hours conflict with your available hours, you may encounter difficulties in scheduling important office visits. Ask about the availability of evening and weekend hours.

❏ *How can I contact you outside of regular office hours?* While an attorney may not be willing to give you his or her home telephone number, a professional attorney will provide alternate methods (voice mail, answering service, pager, beeper, cellular phone) to contact them on evenings, weekends, and holidays.

❏ *How much time do you spend in trial?* A heavy trial schedule may mean that the attorney is not adept at negotiating successful *pre-trial* settlements. Also, when your attorney is in trial on another case, she is often not available to take any action on *your* case. A good attorney will inform you early on of any upcoming trials so that you know her schedule of availability in advance.

❏ *How much of my contact with you will be through a paralegal?* It is unreasonable to expect that a good personal injury attorney will conduct all of the work on your case. Qualified paralegals will probably conduct some of the activity on your case. It is important, however, to clarify in advance how much of your case will be handled by the attorney, and how much by others. You need to know who you will be working with at every point in your case.

❏ *Will you be handling my case, or will it be referred to a subordinate attorney?*
Ah, yes, the old bait and switch routine! You may interview with the top dog at the firm, and after signing the Representation Agreement, find yourself working with the young pup. Ask and find out *before* signing the agreement if the attorney to whom you are speaking will actually handle your case. Get the facts first, and avoid surprises later!

Once you have discovered some of the operational features of the attorney's practice, it's time to talk more precisely about how the attorney will help you, and how much she will charge for that help.

## Clarify Your Expectations

During this initial meeting, you will need to be *proactive* with the attorney. This means that you need to volunteer your own questions and concerns, and make sure that the attorney's answers satisfy you. The attorney needs to hear what you expect from him, and respond with assurances that those expectations will be met.

## Fees and Costs

A typical concern is, *"How much is this going to cost me?"* The amount and manner in which you pay your attorney for handling your settlement can vary from attorney to attorney. This will be covered in the Fee Agreement that you will be asked to sign if you decide to hire an attorney.

## Fee Agreement

Like any other contract, you should read the Fee Agreement in its entirety. Most agreements are fairly standard and include language detailing:

- What the attorney will provide for you.
- A description of appropriate costs and how they will be paid.
- A description of the fee arrangement (i.e., contingency), or how the attorney expects to be paid.
- What is expected of you, the client.
- What will be done in the event of a fee dispute.

If you don't like *any* part of the Fee Agreement, ask the attorney if that section can be deleted. If he declines, *don't sign it*, and consult another attorney to represent you.

Some Fee Agreements are a single page; others are multiple pages with tiny typed legalese. It is important that you read any Fee Agreement in its entirety, and ask the attorney to explain anything you don't understand.

## Contractual Obligations

The Fee Agreement is a contract that you can cancel at any time, for any reason. This means that you can fire your attorney whenever you want to, and you don't even have to explain why. Keep in mind, however, that you will be obligated to pay the attorney for the work that she has put into your case. Most Fee Agreements contain language that covers payment to the attorney in the event you discontinue the representation. If you owe an attorney money for work conducted on your behalf, the attorney will typically place a lien on any settlement amount you receive and get reimbursed when your case settles.

On the other hand, an attorney may dismiss you as a client for good cause. "Good cause" is somewhat hard to prove, and it is the rare attorney who will withdraw from representing you unless he has good reason to do so. If you are abusive or otherwise pose a risk to the attorney or his staff, the attorney would have good cause to withdraw from representing you. If your attorney just doesn't like you, that's not good cause.

The trick to avoiding firing and hiring attorneys (or being "fired" yourself!) is to do your homework *before* signing the Fee Agreement. Attorneys *sell* their ability to represent you. You *buy* that representation. It is a business partnership in every sense of the word, and demands the same consideration and care you would put into forming any other business partnership. If at any time during your relationship with your attorney you are unhappy or dissatisfied, *communicate* with your attorney. A minor misunderstanding or miscommunication shouldn't permanently damage your working relationship. It won't if you keep the lines of communication open.

On the other hand, if you are truly dissatisfied with your attorney's representation, and your efforts to communicate go unanswered and the problems remain unresolved, it's time to move on and find representation that you can work and live with.

## How the Attorney Gets Paid

There are two ways an attorney typically gets paid: either by a contingency fee, or by the hour.

## Contingency Fee

Most personal injury attorneys charge for their legal services on a contingency basis. This means that the attorney takes a certain percentage (usually one-third) of the total settlement proceeds. If you do not win a settlement, the attorney does not charge a fee. Attorneys are willing to take this risk because if they do their job right and negotiate effectively, they will almost certainly be paid for their efforts.

Here is an example of a simple contingency arrangement. Your personal injury attorney has worked diligently on your case and established a high claim value. The insurance company offers to settle your case for $30,000 and writes one check in that amount made out to you and your attorney. Your attorney gets one-third, or $10,000, and you get two-thirds, or $20,000.

Contingency fees can become a little more complex. Let's say you incurred $10,000 in medical bills, and your health insurance company paid all of those medical bills. In your contract with your health insurer, there is language that talks about "subrogation." This means that if your health insurance company pays for medical care you need as a result of the accident, and you obtain settlement money for that accident, your health insurance company may be entitled to full reimbursement.

**The difference between just another insurance settlement and a *good* insurance settlement is often the experienced personal injury attorney who increases the value of your claim significantly with experience, skilled negotiating abilities, and a trained professional staff.**

When you receive the settlement check from the at-fault driver's insurance company, your attorney will receive one-third of $30,000, or $10,000, as her contingency fee. In addition, there are probably $1,500 in costs that the attorney advanced for your case (long distance telephone charges, photocopying, medical reports, etc.) So your attorney receives $11,500, and you will receive $18,500. But your medical insurer will want $10,000 of your share, leaving you with only $6,500.

But wait! A qualified personal injury attorney knows how to work with your health insurer and greatly reduce or completely cancel that $10,000 bill. And you walk away with more money in your pocket than you otherwise would have received.

You may receive $1,500 by settling on your own. But a professional may be able to settle your case for $5,000, which leaves far more money in your pocket *even after attorneys fees are paid*. Your attorney is best qualified to determine the value of your case.

## Hourly Rate

It is *very* unusual for a qualified personal injury attorney to bill you by the hour. In this situation, there is absolutely no incentive for the attorney to produce a higher settlement. Whether you get $5.00 or $5,000, an attorney who bills by the hour gets paid the same. Typically an attorney billing by the hour will not put the same amount of enthusiasm and effort into your case as she would if she stood to earn a contingency with a higher settlement amount.

If an attorney offers to take your personal injury case on an hourly rate, ask him to do it on a contingency basis. If he refuses, consider agreeing to an hourly rate only if you have a written agreement that (1) clearly limits the number of billable hours that will be charged in pursuit of a satisfactory settlement and (2) provides that you will not be billed anything at all if there is no settlement.

## Costs

Every attorney charges for the miscellaneous costs that are incurred for handling your case. These costs may include charges for long distance telephone calls, photocopying, deliveries, depositions, medical reports, videotapes, faxes, postage, court costs, filing fees, jury fees, etc. By law, an attorney cannot pay your costs for you. This could look like a shady deal offered by the attorney to hook your business and is prohibited by rules of professional conduct.

## Simple Advance

Different attorneys collect payment for typical costs in different ways. One way is for the attorney to advance your costs, and be reimbursed when you settle. If your attorney manages costs this way, you will not be expected to pay anything until your case settles. This is your best option, since you are not expected to pay any cash out of your pocket until the settlement check arrives.

Most attorneys who handle costs this way typically have set aside substantial funds of their own to accommodate their clients as they are going through the difficult process of recovery and settlement negotiation. This is a sign of a professional, conscientious, and successful legal practice.

## Advance with Interest

Be wary of this method! The attorney will pay costs as they arise, but will add an *additional* finance charge to the costs at time of settlement. This decreases the portion of settlement money that comes to you, especially if your costs are high.

## Retainer

Some attorneys will ask for a retainer, or a cash deposit, up front, and deposit that money in a trust fund. As your case proceeds, the attorney will withdraw money from the trust fund to pay costs as they are incurred. If the retainer balance is exhausted, the attorney will contact you and request that you deposit additional funds to cover impending costs. This can become a real problem for clients who do not have a steady cash flow due to injuries and employment difficulties. This may be a signal that you should look for another attorney.

## Monthly Billings

Some attorneys will consolidate all of the costs for the month and issue a monthly bill to the client. The client is expected to pay the bill in full each month. This can prove to be burdensome, if not impossible, for someone who has been seriously injured in an automobile accident and is unable to work to generate income.

## Direct Billing

A few attorneys will send bills for costs directly to the client as those costs are incurred. This is probably the most bothersome method for injured clients. Managing a flood of bills demanding payment can be burdensome.

## Trial Costs

Trials cost money — sometimes *lots* of money. They present a substantial investment in time and effort for the attorney. A professional personal injury attorney will discuss anticipated trial costs with you at the onset of representation. If it appears that settlement negotiations have failed and your case is going to trial, most attorneys will require that you advance anticipated trial costs before trial. This is something you must discuss with your attorney *early* in your case. If you are unable to afford a trial, your attorney can discuss and recommend other options, including settlement, arbitration, mediation, or the private court system.

## Communications

Falling right behind the importance of determining "How much is this going to cost me?" come the nuts and bolts of how you're going to work with an attorney. The most important component to a successful working relationship is *communication* between you and your attorney.

When you first meet with an attorney, ask her to explain how the office will handle your case and how the progress of your case will be communicated to you. Some sample questions might be:

## Attorney Communications Checklist

❏ How long do you think this will take to settle?

❏ What is likely to bring about settlement?

❏ If that doesn't happen, what are our options?

❏ How often, and in what manner, will you be communicating with my medical practitioners?

❏ To what extent is my spouse/partner to be involved in my case?

❏ What do you expect of me (time, activities, attendance at meetings)?

❏ Do I need to continue communicating with the insurance company?

❏ What kinds of telephone calls, inquiries, contacts, etc. should I refer to you?

❏ Will you call me with regular status reports? How often?

❏ Will you send me regular written reports? How often?

❏ Will you give me adequate advance notice of any important examinations, interviews, appearances?

❏ Can I see my file whenever I want to?

❏ Will you regularly tell me what the insurance company is doing about my case?

❏ How will you notify me when the insurance company makes a settlement offer?

❏ What am I expected to do when a settlement offer comes in?

❏ How do I control the costs incurred in my case?

❏ What happens if the settlement is less than the costs and fees you're going to charge me?

## Summary

The bad news is, finding the right attorney can be a difficult task, especially if you've been injured in an automobile accident and are undergoing a painful, protracted recovery.

The good news is, if you follow the guidelines in this chapter, do your homework, and keep an open mind and *open ears*, you will surely find the professional personal injury attorney who can provide the support, management, and guidance needed to negotiate or litigate your claim successfully.

You have absolutely nothing to lose by scheduling a free consultation with a qualified personal injury attorney who will review your case and share valuable guidance and advice. Even if you decide to settle your own case after talking to an attorney, you'll have the additional tools and information provided during the free consultation to increase your claim value.

If you follow some of the helpful guidelines presented in this chapter and ultimately decide to hire an attorney to represent you in your personal injury settlement, you will be assured of a productive and successful relationship with your attorney.

As in all business matters, an *informed* consumer is a *satisfied* consumer. Shop carefully, and if you decide to buy, do so wisely. The financial benefits of a successful personal injury settlement are certainly worth an effort on your part to examine all of your options and get as much information as possible from as many different possible sources. Obtaining the guidance and advice of a trained personal injury professional at any step in your negotiation process will "cost" only limited time and effort — and both well spent at that!

## Survival Guide Checklist

❏ If you decide you need an attorney, find the best one.

❏ Be proactive in your search.

❏ Put in the time and effort early on to ensure a good working relationship with your attorney.

❏ Keep the communications lines open with your attorney.

❏ Trust your attorney to give you sound, experienced advice.

# Managing Your
# Medical Care

In Chapter 5, you learned how to find the right attorney to handle your case. In this chapter, we'll
talk about what you need to do to find and manage
the appropriate medical care for your injuries.

## Making Your Way Through the Medical Maze

If you were injured in an automobile accident, you
were most likely transported by ambulance to a
hospital Emergency Room ("ER"). Standard procedure in the ER involves quickly diagnosing your
injuries, giving treatment as required, and determining whether you are facing a life-threatening
condition. You may have been admitted to the hospital under the direct care of a hospital physician,
or discharged with appropriate referrals for follow-
up care by other medical caregivers.

When you were released from the hospital, you
probably got a diagnosis of your injuries. You may
also have been given medication or prosthetic de-

vices, such as a soft leg splint or cervical collar, to alleviate the pain and discomfort of your injuries. The ER physician may have also provided a referral to an appropriate medical specialist for follow-up care. If you already have a relationship with a different medical caregiver with whom you wish to seek follow-up care, the ER physician will direct you to that doctor. In either case, it's important to follow up on the referral and make an appointment for a full examination immediately.

If you experience continued pain, bruising, swelling, inability to move, headaches, nausea, or other worrisome symptoms, or if you suspect that you have injuries that were not diagnosed during your initial visit to the ER before you are able to keep your appointment with the doctor to whom you have been referred, return to the emergency room immediately for follow-up care. While emergency rooms are primarily equipped to handle "life and death" emergencies, you shouldn't hesitate to return to the ER for help with unmanageable pain or discomfort when you can't get immediate help from another source. Your own pain threshold will dictate when and if you go to the ER, but in no case is it expected that you endure unremitting pain or untreated physical disability while you await a scheduled appointment with a doctor outside of the hospital's ER.

## Follow-up Care

Make an appointment immediately to see either the doctor referred by the ER or your personal physician. Some people are comfortable seeing a new doctor recommended by the ER physician. Others are more at ease seeing a doctor they have seen before. In any case, the important thing is to follow-up *now*. If you wait days, weeks or months to seek treatment for injuries received in an automobile accident, you may endanger your health. The chances of your being able to prove that the injuries were caused by the accident grow more remote as time passes.

*Failure to obtain medical treatment and documentation of your injuries immediately following an injury can seriously hurt your settlement efforts.*

During your initial visit, your physician or Chiropractor should interview you thoroughly about the accident and your injuries. He should also review the ER records and X-rays, perform a full examination, provide appropriate diagnoses, and prescribe treatment. This may include a prescription for anti-inflammatory medication, pain medication, or muscle relaxants. The doctor may also recommend a cervical collar or other supporting device if the hospital didn't already give you one.

In many cases your family doctor will refer you to another specialist for additional follow-up care. In all cases, take your examining physician's advice and recommendations to heart and *act on them*. When, six months later, the insurance adjuster casually asks you why you never went to physical therapy as prescribed by your doctor, you'll know then that you just blew a large part of your settlement claim. You likely also jeopardized your physical recovery.

If your doctor or Chiropractor doesn't offer one, ask for a specific treatment time line. That is, your doctor may prescribe ten visits to a physical therapist for treatment of your neck and back injuries and pain. Your Chiropractor may decide that a two-month series of Chiropractic treatments are in order to fully treat your injuries.

**Treatment plans should be communicated to the insurance adjuster so that the insurance company can anticipate and set aside anticipated payments, or *reserves*, for your settlement. There won't be any surprises if the insurance adjuster is kept continually informed of your treatment, especially if your doctor extends or changes the treatment plan.**

## What if I'm Not Recovering?

If after the prescribed term of treatment you have still not reached anticipated recovery, it's time to sit down with the health care provider and discuss the situation. Is more of this type of treatment required? Should you consider alternative treatments? Is there something you should be doing that you haven't been doing to hasten recovery? Is there something else going on here, perhaps an undiagnosed injury, that may be interfering with your recovery under this treatment plan? These are all issues you should discuss with your health care provider.

Communicating your concerns and your desire for full recovery with your treatment provider will en-

130

courage open discussion of your situation and the options that are available to you. Usually, your treatment provider will be enthusiastic about redesigning an appropriate plan of treatment for you. Perhaps a different approach to physical therapy is in order. Alternatively, he may refer you to another specialist for a second opinion and an opportunity to evaluate and modify your current treatment plan.

The worst case scenario would be your doctor shrugging his shoulders and saying, "I don't know what to do." If this happens, *you* need to take the initiative and suggest that you see another specialist who may have an alternative treatment plan that will hasten your recovery. Your primary goal must be full physical recovery. If you are not getting that with your present treatment provider within a reasonable period of time, it's time for you to be proactive and seek alternatives.

Some people become very comfortable with one doctor. Perhaps they've been seeing this particular doctor forever and hesitate to make a change. Maybe the patient is afraid of insulting the doctor by asking to see someone for a second opinion. As in the field of law, doctors specialize in different areas of practice. No matter how much you trust him, it doesn't make any sense to continue to see your gynecologist for treatment of a back injury.

Nor does it make much sense to continue to see a doctor who has not been able to provide successful treatment of your injuries. This can happen if your particular injury and treatment needs fall outside of the specialty of the doctor you have been seeing. In this situation, your doctor should refer you to a specialist who has more experience with your type of injury.

If you make the decision to seek alternate treatment of your injuries, communicate your decision to your doctor and reach a mutual decision about the referral. Once a doctor has participated in your plan for recovery, you want to keep that doctor on your medical team until you have reached maximum medical improvement ("MMI") and have successfully settled your claim. Even after the doctor has stopped treating your injuries, you may need to return to that doctor later for other treatment or referrals. Also, you may need to ask that doctor for medical records or testimony for your settlement claim.

Direct, clear communication is going to make any treatment changes or decisions a team effort between the two of you. Coming out of the blue with a spontaneous demand that you see another doctor will likely surprise and possibly alienate your medical caregiver. Open communication can prevent detrimental surprises.

### *Don't* Shop Until You Drop!

There's a big difference between seeking the most appropriate care and shopping indiscriminately for a doctor, *any* doctor. This may later look like you were on the hunt for a doctor who would provide an inflated diagnosis of your injuries and support a higher value for your claim. Seeking *appropriate* care is a legitimate and justifiable effort on your part to successfully manage optimal recovery. *Indiscriminate doctor shopping is fraud!*

Medical, legal, and insurance professionals are experts at identifying claimants who are trying to work the system for financial gain. You'll be wasting the valuable time of everyone involved and you'll irretrievably damage your case if your actions represent anything less than total commitment to finding the right medical care. Appropriate care will provide the best chances of recovery from your injuries.

Your medical history should display a conscientious effort to seek out and employ the services of medical professionals who can assist you in reaching maximum recovery. Diligently follow prescribed treatment plans before making any changes. Your record will clearly show that your treatment plan was in the best interests of your physical recovery and was not designed to abuse the system for financial recovery.

Worse yet, if your medical history shows a wide range of unrelated, inconsistent complaints to different doctors at different times, or if there is no verifiable medical proof to back up your claims, your demand for settlement may appear suspect and be summarily refused by the insurance company. Professional personal injury attorneys are likely to decline to represent clients who doctor shop because they suggest either a poorly documented and losing case or an attempt to commit insurance fraud.

**It is your right and it is your *responsibility* to seek out the best possible care and treatment, even if it means seeing many doctors. But avoid accumulating a medical history that shows that you have jumped from one doctor to another, or from one treatment to another, without any commitment on your part to follow prescribed treatment plans and truly seek recovery. Your claims will become suspect and immediately diminish.**

Your records need to show, and your physical condition should demonstrate, that all of the treatment by all of the providers was *reasonable* and *necessary*. *Reasonable* means that the treatment was provided for an appropriate amount of time and cost; *necessary* means that the treatment was referred and monitored by the attending physician. Without adequate proof of these two qualifying conditions, a long shopping list of medical treatment may be successfully refuted by the insurance company or its lawyers.

## Managing Your Recovery

If you are injured in an automobile accident, you are on a two-lane road to recovery: both physical and financial. Your primary concern should be your physical recovery. Your choice of a medical team, and their subsequent management of your medical care, will play a large part in your physical recovery. It's helpful to find a medical caregiver who will become your primary care provider and manage the progress of your case and recovery. Remember, though, that at every step of your care, *you* are the ultimate manager of your recovery and it is you who must assume the primary responsibility for a healthful recuperation and recovery.

This is not to say that while you are working on your physical recovery, you should completely ignore your financial recovery. On the contrary, it's important that you find the best way to manage the *physical* aspects of your recovery so that the time and effort it takes to perform the *financial management* side of your recovery does not interfere with your ability to get on with your life. When you have accomplished this balance, you will be able to manage your physical recovery while accomplishing everything you need to do to return to the financial condition you would have been in had you not been injured.

With a perfect mix of caring and conscientious caregivers and your executive management skills, you may have little to worry about when it comes to managing your physical and financial recovery.

However, in the real world, doctors specializing in different areas of practice don't customarily communicate with each other about your care. The truth is, your dentist has little incentive to regularly call your Chiropractor for periodic updates on your recovery. And when you're trying to coordinate a variety of appointments from one end of town to the other, mustering all of the appropriate medical records, paying the bills, calling the insurance company, struggling to return to work full-time and doing all of this *on crutches*, your skillful management of both your physical recovery and your financial recovery may prove elusive or impossible.

If you choose to hire an attorney to assist you in managing your full recovery, your attorney will assume the most important duties of managing your medical care. Many people injured in an automobile accident find it difficult to assume full responsibility for medical care management. If you find that you are unable to competently or comfortably manage your health care, you should consider hiring an attorney to assume the comprehensive management of all aspects of your case, including your physical and financial recovery.

*You* are the best and only judge of whether or not you are up to the task. If you feel that you are, and you're *not* experiencing increased stress or frustration that hampers your physical recovery, then you are a good candidate for managing your own case. If, however, you have doubts about your ability to adequately manage both your physical and financial recovery, or you suspect that the time and effort needed to do it well is exacting a heavy toll on your recovery, it's time to ask for professional help.

## Communicating with Your Medical Caregivers

Whether you are seeing your family doctor, a referred caregiver, or an ER physician for treatment of your injuries, you need to communicate clearly and consistently with the doctor about your injuries and the effects those injuries have on your physical well-being.

Your first communication with a doctor will be a thorough and detailed description of your injuries, including how you received them and what their impact has been on you. You should discuss the effects of those injuries on your health, your expectations for physical recovery, and your responsibilities in the treatment plan. Full disclosure of everything about your injuries is very important at the onset. The treatment plan prescribed by the doctor at this point will depend a great deal on what you communicate during your first visit.

It is important to discuss the following with your health care providers:

### Health Care Provider Communications Checklist

❑ Can you treat my injuries?

❑ What treatment do you advise?

❑ Is there anything I shouldn't be doing during treatment (lifting, working, running)?

❏ How long should my treatment continue?

❏ What happens if the treatment doesn't work?

❏ Is surgery required?

❏ Will you refer me to another doctor if necessary?

❏ Will I fully recover from my injuries?

❏ If not, what will be my limitations?

❏ What do I need to do to fully participate in the treatment plan now?

❏ What might I need to do in the future to continue treating this injury?

❏ Will you be available to work with me (or my attorney) in my settlement negotiations?

## Managing Your Medical Records

At every step of your physical recovery, your communication with your attending physicians will most likely make their way into the medical charts. These charts become the official record of the effects of your injury, the care given to treat your injury, and your recovery from the injury.

During settlement negotiations with the insurance company, the medical charts and records that your doctors create provide the foundation both for your claim and the insurance company's defense. If your injuries and their impact on you are officially noted in your medical records, there is sound evidence to prove your claim of injury, pain, and suffering. This works to your advantage.

However, if you submit a claim for injuries that are *not* noted anywhere in the medical records, or if your own claims and assertions differ from the observations, diagnoses, and treatments recorded by your medical caregivers, the insurance company will move quickly to dismiss those claims.

Every time you speak to a medical caregiver, you should provide a full and candid explanation of your injuries and how those injuries have affected you. Without proof of injury, pain, and suffering evidenced by official medical records, you may well be left without any evidence to support your claims.

Ongoing communications with the insurance adjustor are also important. Your regular and comprehensive reports of your physical and financial condition document the extent and severity of the injuries and the pain and suffering you are experiencing as a result. Your reports also keep the insurance company informed on a timely basis about the nature of your injuries and your anticipated recovery from them.

## Involving the Whole Medical Team

Having said this, does it make sense to tell your dentist about the headaches you've been experiencing each morning? Yes! Your dentist has the professional experience and training to assist with a diagnosis of injury to your jaw and the surrounding tissues that may have been caused by trauma to your head, neck, or back in the automobile accident. In this case, she would probably make a referral to an appropriate physician for follow-up care.

Should you tell your Chiropractor about the grinding noise in your left knee that suddenly appeared a few days after the accident? Definitely! While you may be seeing your Chiropractor for treatment of your head, neck, and back injuries, he is an expert on the mechanics of how the impact of an automobile collision can cause trauma to many different parts of the body. The grinding in your knee may well have been caused by extending your leg to slam the brake pedal at the moment when you collided with thousands of pounds of high-speed metal. Such tremendous forces can cause serious injury to your knee and other parts of your body as well.

**The information contained in your medical records is one of the most important components of the total documentation package that will support your settlement claim.** *Everything matters.*

When you return to the neurologist for a follow-up appointment one month after your original appointment with her, is it really necessary to again recite the entire litany of your injuries and the pain, problems, and limitations you have been experiencing? Absolutely! *You can't communicate too much to your medical caregivers.* Something that may not have found its way onto your medical chart during one appointment can always be added to your records by your doctor during a later appointment.

Keep in mind, also, that the typical medical practitioner may have hundreds, if not thousands, of other patients with their own medical histories and complaints. It's simply too much to expect that a doctor will remember your entire history each time he steps into the examining room to see you. The doctor's demanding appointment schedule may allow only a cursory review of the medical records contained in your chart. It's up to you to fill in the blanks and make sure that everything about your injuries and your recovery is communicated to your doctor and included in your medical records. This is very important if you are to successfully manage your injury and treatment.

## Managing Multiple Caregivers

The more extensive your injuries, the more likely it is that you will be seeing more than one medical caregiver. Customarily, you will be referred to doctors who specialize in the particular area in which you have been injured. For example, you may be referred to an orthopedic specialist for a fractured tibia, to a dentist for broken teeth, to a neurologist for a closed head injury and concussion, to a Chiropractor for neck and back sprain, and to a psychotherapist for treatment of post-traumatic stress and depression.

In this incredible mix of specialties, you may feel that your body is composed of mutually exclusive territories, where one doctor may venture for diagnosis and treatment, but where another won't dare to tread. Throughout your medical care, however, you need to remember that your body and your health are combined into one comprehensive, albeit complex unit.

**The healing of your body and your mind is a team effort between all of your medical caregivers.**

While it may seem that the various doctors have exclusive rights to your various bits and pieces, *you* are the manager of the whole business, and it's *your* responsibility to make sure that everyone — from Chiropractor to psychotherapist — understands the nature of all of your injuries.

When you communicate well with all of your caregivers, you are in effect giving each of them the opportunity to apply their wide-ranging experience and skill to your full recovery. If you limit your communications and share only part of your injury history with some of the doctors, your whole medical team suffers for lack of complete information and total understanding of your condition.

When it comes time to settle your case, if your medical records show that you have consistently and clearly communicated to your attending physicians about your injuries and their impact on you, and your caregivers in turn have responded appropriately with diagnoses and treatment, the value of your case is increased dramatically. On the other hand, nonexistent or incomplete medical records mean that your injuries and the value of your case can be misinterpreted by the insurance company. If there are any uncertainties about your claim, insurance companies are not very likely to give *you* the benefit of the doubt!

## Traditional vs. Alternative Medical Care

America in the '90s is home to some of the most progressive and technologically superior medical care available in the world. It is not unusual for an injured person to receive professional care from a medical team composed of an emergency room physician, the family doctor, a radiologist, a Chiropractor, a hypnotherapist, and an acupuncturist. As the demand for a variety of successful treatment options continues to grow, it's becoming more and more common to find that traditional medical care shares clinic space with more alternative forms of medicine.

## Chiropractic

More and more people are opting for less traditional modes of medical care. Some people still think of Chiropractic as a "nontraditional" method of medical care. However, in the past few decades, Chiropractic has grown in popularity and acceptance among patients and traditional medical practitioners alike.

Some Chiropractors will treat only neck and back problems and injuries, and some people continue to see their Chiropractor for these reasons only. Many more people, however, view their Chiropractor as their primary health provider. These Chiropractors provide comprehensive physical care for their patients beyond the treatment of back and neck problems and injuries.

 **Some health insurance plans do not cover Chiropractic care, especially if you are unable to obtain a referral for Chiropractic from your attending physician. Costs for reasonable and necessary Chiropractic care are, however, reimbursable at the time of your insurance settlement.**

Many people prefer Chiropractic over more traditional medical care because by its very nature, Chiropractic is more of a "hands on" method of health care. The Chiropractor will manually touch, massage, and manipulate your spine and related muscles and tissues to achieve maximum alignment and healthy interaction. Chiropractors tend to look at the whole picture and treat your symptoms based on a larger view of what is going on with your body and overall health. Chiropractors are not licensed to dispense prescription medications, and many patients prefer this more natural approach to healing. On the other hand, your Chiropractor will refer you to a

144

medical practitioner in the event she diagnoses a condition for which you require treatment or medications outside of the scope of Chiropractic.

Medical reports generated by your Chiropractor are considered by the insurance adjuster as a very important part of your overall medical history. Records of your care submitted by your Chiropractor are customarily extensive, detailed, and comprehensive. They are a valuable part of your settlement package, and will speak clearly to neck, back, and other injuries you received in the automobile accident.

Whether you choose to include your Chiropractor on your medical team for treatment of your neck and back injuries only, or if you decide to have your Chiropractor provide comprehensive medical care and act as your primary physician, it's important to incorporate your Chiropractic care with all of your other medical treatments. Your neurologist will probably not make a direct referral to a Chiropractor, because there is very little cross practice interaction between the two professions. That is why you need to take the initiative and ask your attending physician to invite your Chiropractor onto your team of medical providers and make her an active participant in your total recovery.

## Holistic Alternatives

Other alternative methods may include acupuncture, herbal remedies, homeopathic treatment, and massage therapy. While your treatment provider may not spontaneously refer you to one of these alternative specialties, do not hesitate to suggest these treatments as reasonable alternatives to a traditional treatment plan.

If you have knowledge of the effectiveness of an alternative form of medicine and communicate a sincere desire to apply it to your physical recovery, your treatment provider will most likely agree with your suggested plan of action. Your doctor may not give an enthusiastic blessing to this new treatment plan, but it is unlikely that a doctor who is truly concerned with your recovery will obstruct your commitment to find healing treatment, wherever your search may lead.

**Your health insurance plan may not cover some alternative medical treatments. If, however, you are able to prove at the time of settlement that alternative treatments provided relief and aided in your physical recovery, you will most likely be able to receive reimbursement for such treatments as a part of your settlement. The insurance company should provide reimbursement for all medical care that is reasonable and necessary.**

If you decide to seek alternative care, make sure that you communicate your desire to your attending physician so that her agreement with your decision is noted in the medical records. Also, make sure that you report the outcome of the alternative treatment to your attending physician, especially if it is positive. A report from an herbalist will probably not be included in the official medical records used by the insurance company to assess your claim. However, your attending physician's reference in your medical chart to successful treatment by the herbalist is a valuable component of your overall medical record.

## Maximum Medical Improvement

It's important to reach maximum medical improvement (MMI) before settling your claim with the insurance company. MMI is achieved when your physical condition is fixed and stable. Treatment may be available that provides *temporary relief*, but a finding of MMI means that there is no treatment available that will permanently *change* or *improve* your condition at that point.

*Agreeing to a settlement before you know your final physical outcome is a tremendous risk.*

Why should you wait until you have reached MMI before settling? Following injury in an automobile accident, any number of things can occur. You may find that two *weeks* after the accident, you have no lasting injuries or problems from the injury, and your physician declares full recovery. If so, celebrate your marvelous good fortune and rest assured that your claim will most likely be settled quickly.

Alternatively, you may find that two *years* after the accident you are still unable to work or function at the level you could before the accident. *Time* is the great equalizer of injuries suffered in an accident. It is only after a sufficient amount of time, with appropriate treatment of your injuries and careful monitoring of your recovery, that you will have a

**AVOID DELAYS**

*The more serious the injuries, the more important it is to wait until you reach MMI before even considering a settlement with the insurance company. If an extended wait is causing financial hardship, or damage to your quality of life, or mental or emotional difficulties, or is just plain wearing you down, it's time to get an attorney on your side who will help you back onto the right track of physical and financial recovery.*

clear idea of how serious and perhaps how permanently disabling your injuries may be.

When you're overwhelmed with pain and disability, medical bills, insurance forms to fill out, phone calls to return, unemployment worries and all the other things that seem to pile up after an automobile accident, it's really tempting to jump at a chance for early settlement. The insurance companies know (and conduct a large part of their business based on this knowledge) that the typical claimant will just want to get the whole settlement process over with and settle quickly. But until you have *fully* recovered, a hasty settlement is the *worst* possible thing you can do.

Until your medical team provides you with a final determination of your medical prognosis, you have absolutely no way of knowing when or even if your injuries will fully heal. There's no way to know if or when you will return to the condition you were in before the accident.

Let's say you settle for $15,000 three months after the accident for head, neck, and back injuries. As a condition of the early settlement, you sign a release that exempts the insurance company from any further obligation to pay for medical care incurred because of the accident.

Imagine this frightening scenario: Four months after the accident, your arms begin growing numb. The next day, you are in the hospital for major emergency surgery to remove disk fragments and repair damaged nerves in your neck. Five months after the accident, you are undergoing intensive rehabilitation for your partial and *permanent paralysis.*

Your world just caved in on you. Where are you going to look for payment of thousands of dollars in medical bills? Who is going to support your family? Who is going to reimburse you for the loss of your ability to walk, run, play, and work? The answer: nobody. Because if you settle too early, before obtaining a complete analysis and determination of your physical health and recovery, you've burned any bridge between you and full financial recovery. The results could be disastrous for your life, and for your family's future as well.

**Your physical recovery is the most important aspect of any insurance settlement claim**

Don't compromise your physical recovery by the temptation of an early settlement. Trust your medical team to provide the best possible care and make the most professional and educated determinations of your physical status. Don't be left holding a bag of woefully insignificant cash if your recovery falters. The quality of your life and your financial future may be damaged beyond recovery by an early, insufficient settlement.

Your medical team has the experience and expertise to determine your physical status and the prognosis, or medical prediction, of full recovery at any phase during your recuperation. The insurance companies are highly skilled at interpreting the medical reports to make an assessment of the value of your claim based on the medical prognosis. And somewhere in between, *you* (or your attorney) assume the full responsibility for translating the medical prognosis into a reasonable settlement for your injuries, pain, and suffering.

## Being the Good Patient

Developing the "good patient" in yourself is almost as important as finding good medical caregivers and developing them into a successful medical care giving team. There are a few characteristics that you'll need to develop if you want to create the most productive and successful relationship with your medical team.

**Attitude**. Believe that you'll recover. Don't climb up on the treadmill muttering to yourself, "This isn't going to work." And if you need psychological help to reach this belief, get it.

**Discipline**. Follow the treatment plan prescribed by your doctor to the letter, and for as long as the doctor has prescribed it. If the doctor says "no tennis," then put the racket away. If the doctor says "walk a mile every day," then pull out those walking shoes and start moving.

**Commitment**. When you and your medical team have designed your treatment plan, commit to it with all the physical, mental, and emotional resources you have. Set a recovery goal, and stick to it. Ask your family and friends for their support. Prepare for the ups and downs of your recovery, and don't let minor, or even major setbacks steer you off course. If you find that your commitment is wavering, get a professional coach (your attorney) to help you.

**Be your own best friend during recovery. Follow the plan, work with it, and make it work *for* you.**

**Consistency**. The worst thing you can do to your health as you're recovering from your auto accident is to jump on the recovery trampoline. Saturday you feel better than you ever have since the accident, so you corral the dog and go on a ten-mile uphill climb. Sunday, you can't get out of bed because you've re-strained your lower back. You spend the next two weeks in intensive physical therapy, right back on square one.

**Balance**. This is probably the most elusive and challenging characteristic. You need to balance your life with your treatment plan. Your life probably already includes family, work, friends, social commitments, and civic responsibilities. Add to this mix the complex settlement negotiations with an insurance company. If you can't balance the whole picture, you're going to lose a lot of focus. And if you can't balance everything, ask for help.

## Summary

Just when you thought the insurance industry was a scary place to be, you've now entered *the medical zone!* Yes, it can be frustrating and frightening and sometimes a little bit painful. But when you work together and consistently communicate with your medical caregivers to design a treatment plan, and you commit yourself to that plan and set your sights on full physical recovery, you'll be amazed at the results that at first you may have thought would be impossible.

Achieving physical and financial recovery is the ultimate balancing act. At a time when your physical and financial resources may be at their lowest possible level, you will be called upon to devote increasing time, effort, and expense to manage your insurance settlement claim.

The key word here is *team*: everyone is involved in the job of getting you back to where you were before the accident. The only way to make that team work to its fullest potential is to manage it carefully, diligently, and skillfully. It's *your* responsibility to make sure that team management stays on track. If you are unable or unwilling to put the time and effort into managing your team, then your physical, emotional, mental, and *financial* survival depends on your hiring someone to step in and do it for you.

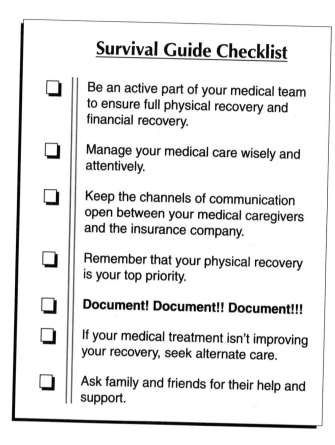

# Survival Guide Checklist

☐ Be an active part of your medical team to ensure full physical recovery and financial recovery.

☐ Manage your medical care wisely and attentively.

☐ Keep the channels of communication open between your medical caregivers and the insurance company.

☐ Remember that your physical recovery is your top priority.

☐ **Document! Document!! Document!!!**

☐ If your medical treatment isn't improving your recovery, seek alternate care.

☐ Ask family and friends for their help and support.

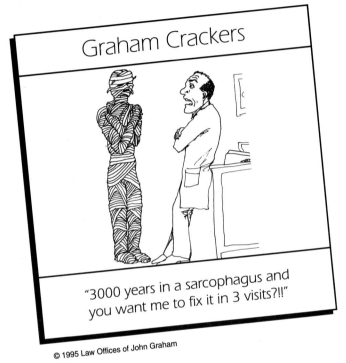

# Personal Injury and Lifestyle Changes

We talked earlier in this book about managing the treatment for your injuries. Physical pain, mental exhaustion, emotional stress, and the financial setbacks of recovery and recuperation shouldn't stop you from conducting successful settlement negotiations and obtaining maximum financial compensation for your losses. In this chapter, we'll talk about some of the physical, mental, and emotional challenges that may arise after you're injured in an automobile accident. We'll review how to identify and document their effects on your life and incorporate your results into successful settlement negotiations.

## The True Impact of an Automobile Accident

Few are the lucky ones who survive an automobile collision without any injuries. The potential for injury, even when automobiles collide at relatively low speed, means that the risk of being injured in an automobile accident is fairly high. Insurance industry statistics say that the average American will be in an automobile accident *once every seven years.*

If this is true, why aren't there millions of people demanding insurance settlements on any given day? The number of people who even initiate a claim for an insurance settlement is only a fraction of the actual number of people injured in automobile accidents. And the number of folks who successfully negotiate insurance settlements that fairly compensate them for all of their losses is an even *smaller* fraction of those initiating claims in the first place.

So what's going on here? Could it be that people are being miraculously healed of their automobile accident injuries? Or are insurance companies gladly and quickly paying accident victims full compensation for all of their losses, generously saving everyone the hassle and anxiety of filing a claim and pursuing settlement negotiations? Or could there be some other force at work here?

The explanation for this imbalance between the large number of people who are injured in automobile accidents, and the much smaller number of people who pursue and receive equitable insurance settlements, is simple: most people who are injured do not have the physical, mental, and emotional strength to successfully battle the insurance giants. Some give up immediately and decide not to even bother filing a claim with the insurance company. Others decide to negotiate a settlement, but are quickly worn down and burned out early in the negotiations by a combination of their injuries and the insurance company experts who know just where to apply the pressure to obtain early and minimal settlement.

If you've already committed to a well-managed plan of successful treatment and an effective settlement strategy, then you are *precisely* the person who can benefit most from the information contained in this chapter. Some attention paid now to maintaining your physical, emotional, and mental strength is going to pay off in the long run. You owe it to yourself to learn how you can best protect your existing personal resources. Now is the time to reinforce and rebuild your total health to reach full physical and financial recovery in the future.

## Physical Injuries

Following an automobile accident, physical injuries can take many forms. Broken bones, bruises, and lacerations are usually immediately visible either to the naked eye or from imaging technology like X-rays or MRI. These visible injuries can be clearly documented by your medical team and often prove to be the most treatable kinds of injuries. They are the most easily identified injuries and are readily accessible and responsive to treatment plans.

Less obvious and quite often more difficult to treat are the invisible injuries, especially soft tissue injuries that may not be evidenced by irrefutable, tangible proof. A sprained muscle, torn ligaments,

157

cervical strain, and some closed-head injuries are examples of serious physical damage to your body that can be difficult to quickly diagnose or document with the kind of obvious, graphic proof that can be provided for a broken leg.

**Often it's not until several hours or sometimes several days after the accident that the debilitating effects of some injuries make themselves known. And they often make themselves known with severe pain, impaired mobility, and partial or total disability.**

Automobile accidents often result in soft tissue injuries. The exaggerated twisting, jerking, and distortion of your head, neck, and spine upon sudden impact causes tremendous forces to act on the delicate neuro-muscular system that supports your body's structural framework. Immediately after the collision, the shock and sudden jolt of adrenaline into your system may keep you from immediately feeling the effects of this incredible assault on your body.

## Injuries to the Head and Brain

Injuries to the head, spine, or neck can disrupt and damage the fragile neurological system that controls all of your bodily activities and functions. The same traumatic stresses that can seriously injure your neck, spine, or other parts of your body can also induce serious injuries to the head and brain. Sometimes injuries to the head are obvious because of bruises, cuts, or fractures of the face or skull. Other injuries to the head area may not be immediately visible at the time of the accident. Bruising, swelling, bleeding, or tearing of the brain and related membranes may not be evident at first.

*A head injury may seriously compromise your ability to successfully manage your settlement negotiations. If your doctor has diagnosed a head injury, consult a personal injury attorney immediately to adequately represent you and manage your settlement negotiations for you.*

These injuries can cause extremely serious and debilitating symptoms that can have a profound effect on the quality of your life after an automobile accident. Injuries to the head and brain require immediate and intense treatment and ongoing care to ensure maximum recovery. Medical science is discovering that even seemingly minor injuries to the head and brain can result in permanent disability. Following an automobile accident, the ER physician performs a minimal examination to identify, diagnose, and treat any life threatening head injuries. As with other sometimes invisible injuries, trauma to the head sometimes goes undetected until some time after the injury-causing accident.

Injuries to other parts of the brain can affect cognitive, or thinking abilities. Your ability to think about many things at once, or to compute complex reasoning problems, or to remember how to perform certain tasks, may be affected by these injuries. People who receive even a minor head injury will often be disoriented for a period of time after the injury. Your doctor will determine if the disorientation is temporary, perhaps because of a concussion, or if it is more serious and requires continued treatment.

The complexities, confusion, and frustration that often accompany insurance settlement negotiations are expected though unfortunate elements of the whole insurance claim process. If you're feeling overwhelmed by these new responsibilities and duties, don't assume that it's a symptom of an as yet undiagnosed head injury! Talk to your doctor about your situation, and ask your doctor to suggest ways to identify the source of your difficulties and improve your ability to function.

Specific brain injuries may also result in problems with muscular coordination, vision, speech, or your senses of taste, smell, and touch. The brain is an extraordinarily complex organ, and only a qualified specialist can adequately diagnose and treat a brain injury.

If you or your primary physician suspect any type of head injury, it is extremely important to see a specialist immediately for further diagnosis and treatment. Head injuries, especially if left undiagnosed and untreated, can create frustrating and sometimes permanent disabilities that may demand significant financial resources for a lifetime.

A well-managed medical team provides the most comprehensive rehabilitative treatment available. Working in conjunction with them, you will likely achieve MMI as targeted. But until you do reach full recovery, you will in all likelihood experience some negative physical effects from the injury. Often, these physical disabilities, whether temporary or permanent, are accompanied by emotional trauma as well.

## The Other Side of Physical Injury: Depression

Emotional distress or depression can be clearly linked with an earlier physical injury. If you're injured in an automobile accident, you may face temporary or permanent physical pain and disability. You may be unable to work for an extended period of time. The everyday lifestyle and financial position that you and your family enjoyed before the accident is suddenly disrupted and may be changed forever. And let's face it: being in a bad automobile accident is a scary experience. It's not unusual for accident survivors to have upsetting nightmares about the accident, or even experience distressingly vivid flashbacks during waking hours.

Studies have determined that depression may be caused by emotional, mental, and physical stress or trauma. If a diagnosis of depression is made by a qualified physician, it is important to communicate this with all of the members of your medical team so that all aspects of your treatment plan can adequately address this condition.

Stressful and debilitating emotional repercussions from an automobile accident can range from a simple reluctance to drive an automobile in heavy traffic to an abject terror of leaving the house at all for fear of further injury or disability. Compounding these stresses are the added pressures of managing your medical care, paying your medical bills, maintaining a progressive treatment plan, deflecting financial disaster, and negotiating an insurance settlement.

Some automobile accident victims are so traumatized by their painful experience that they find themselves just shutting down emotionally. They become unable to handle even the simplest day-to-day tasks. Taking out the garbage, frying an egg for breakfast, or even just walking the dog can be the daily obligation that sends you right over the stress threshold and marks the onset of post-accident emotional trauma and depression.

Radical mood swings can also be caused by severe depression resulting from physical injury. *Physical injuries are treated differently than depression. It's important to seek and receive appropriate medical diagnosis and care to learn the cause of your changing moods.*

## How Do I Know if I'm Depressed?

The nature of depressive illness takes many forms. The information contained in this section is not intended in any way to provide a comprehensive discussion of depression or other emotional responses to the trauma of an automobile accident. The checklist provided below is intended to help you decide if you need professional treatment.

162

If you answer "yes" to any of the questions below, consult your primary physician *immediately* and seek referral to a qualified mental health professional who can devise a treatment plan with you.

## Depression Checklist

❏ Do you find it difficult or impossible to keep a sense of humor about things?

❏ Do you find yourself unable to enjoy the things that you used to enjoy?

❏ Are you sleeping much less or much more than you did before the accident?

❏ Has your appetite changed noticeably since the accident? Have you gained or lost weight?

❏ Do you seem to care less about your personal appearance than before the accident?

❏ Has your consumption of alcohol or other drugs increased since the accident?

❏ Are family, friends, or co-workers suggesting that you're just not the "same old you"?

❏ Are you getting short-tempered, angry, or hostile with family, friends, or co-workers?

❏ Do you find yourself upset or crying over minor situations, or for no apparent reason?

*Only a qualified medical practitioner can determine if you are at risk for or are presently suffering from depression or a related illness.*

❏ Is your work performance suffering because you just can't seem to get the job done?

❏ Do the simplest tasks seem impossible to do (making phone calls, grocery shopping, preparing meals, handling errands)?

❏ Do you find yourself thinking negative thoughts about yourself or your situation in life?

❏ Do you avoid family and friends, preferring to be alone?

❏ Do you ever think about hurting yourself or others?

If any one of the above describes how you're feeling now, seek qualified medical help *today* and make sure that every aspect of your recovery is included in your overall treatment plan.

**Left untreated, emotional stress and depression can quickly lead to *physical* illness that will interfere with your ability to fully recover from your accident.**

The emotional injuries caused by physical trauma are real. The good news is, they are also treatable. If you or your medical team suspect that the stress of your accident is causing depression or any other disabling condition, seek a referral to a qualified mental health professional *immediately*.

## Documenting the Effects of the Accident on Your Employment

Most people injured — whether physically, mentally, or emotionally — in an automobile accident are employed at the time of the accident. Some of these folks are able to return to work immediately after the accident with little or no interruption. Others are not so lucky, and face continued medical treatment and prolonged physical recovery that either limits or entirely prevents them from returning to work.

If your doctor has ordered you to limit or discontinue working, immediately provide a written copy of the doctor's order to the insurance company. This puts the insurance company on notice that you will be claiming reimbursement for lost wages. A typical physician's order will include date of the injury, nature of the injury, why you should limit or discontinue working, and the expected date of your return to part- or full-time employment.

---

**If your doctor's order changes at any time, either shortening or extending the limitations on your ability to work, notify the insurance company immediately.**

---

While you are recovering from your injury, it's important to document *every single minute* that you are unable to work because of the injury. If you are employed, the insurance company will eventually request that your employer provide copies of your time sheets or other attendance records to verify

165

your claims of inability to work and the resulting lost wages. Don't depend solely on your employer's records, however. Keep your own personal record of dates and times when you are unable to work because of pain, disability, or attendance at medical appointments. Include copies of this record with your claim for lost wage reimbursement.

If you customarily worked a forty hour week plus ten hours of overtime each week before the accident, but are only able to work 35 hours each week after the accident, document this fact with copies of your time sheets before and after the accident. Time records indicating a 35-hour work week after the accident may not accurately reflect the fact that your ability to work overtime was reduced dramatically and your income suffered following the accident.

Provide additional written documentation other than your official time sheet that specifically references the difference between your pre- and post-accident total hours worked. A letter from your employer stating that before the accident you were always available and willing to work overtime, but after the accident you weren't even able to put in a 40-hour week, will clearly support your claims for wage loss.

## If You're Self-Employed

If you are self-employed, documenting your damages may be more difficult. To justify the claim that your ability to work was affected by the accident, you will have to produce documentation that provides sufficient proof that you worked a relatively steady number of hours or earned a consistent living during the period preceding the accident. You don't have the luxury of dropping by the company payroll department for official copies of your employment records. You'll be responsible for identifying, organizing, and producing the documentation that verifies your own employment history.

No amount of insistence from you that you "planned" on getting a job soon, or "hoped" to make more money from your business, or "anticipated" getting a raise *were it not for the automobile accident* will convince the insurance company that you suffered compensable wage loss. You must have solid, factual documentation to back up your claim.

Gather copies of contracts and agreements that you have with past, current, and future clients. Project proposals, even if they didn't result in a contract agreement with a client, may be useful as well. They present a good picture of how much work you were actively soliciting and were prepared to do, and how much you would have earned from the work, had you not been limited by the accident.

If you are claiming that you were unable to complete a proposed project because of the accident, you will need to provide solid verification from your doctor stating that you were unable to physically conduct the proposed work because of your injuries. Also provide verification from the potential client stating that they would have hired you had it not been for your inability to work because of the accident.

**You'll need to obtain official verification from your employer (or provide documentation from your own files if you're self-employed) that matches each one of your wage loss claims.**

*As in most every other financial area, the self-employed face added burdens of proof and documentation. If you're self-employed, you may need the help of an attorney to counteract what may become exhaustive demands by the insurance company to prove your wage loss claims.*

Ask your clients for letters verifying that you performed certain services and how much time you took to complete each project. Better yet, prepare letters for them so that all they need to do is add their signature. Invoices or billing statements from before and after the accident should also be included in your documentation to show how your income decreased after the accident. Start by providing a six-month review of your self-employment history. The insurance company may ask for an even longer history, but you can respond to such requests as they arise.

Submit copies of the Profit and Loss Statements or Business Plans that you use for financial planning to substantiate your claims of damage to your business. Refer to bank loan or line of credit applications for additional, verifiable proof of your financial status before and after the accident. Be prepared for the insurance company to ask for copies of your bank deposits to verify your income claims.

168

## How Do I Prove Damages?

When you're documenting your wage loss and other damages, you need to be precise about the dollar amounts that you are claiming. *The only way to effectively <u>prove</u> your case is to provide irrefutable <u>facts</u>.* Following are some guidelines to help you determine a reasonable and equitable claim and how to support it.

### Wage Loss Checklist

You must provide proof of:

❏ How much money you earned each pay period during the six months before the accident.

❏ How much money you earned each pay period following the accident, to date.

❏ How many hours you worked each pay period during the six months before the accident.

❏ How many hours you worked each pay period following the accident, to date.

❏ Document any anticipated raises, promotions, cost-of-living, or performance-based salary increases that you lost because of the accident.

❏ List all employment-related benefits, reimbursements, bonuses, profit sharing, sales commissions, gifts, or awards that you would have received had you continued to work at your pre-injury level.

❏ List all employment-related medical,
employment, or other insurance benefits that
you may have lost or needed to pay for out-
of-pocket because of your inability to work.

❏ Provide medical records documenting the
anticipated date of your return to work.

## Documenting How the Injury Affects Your Ability to Work

*How* you are able to perform your work is related
to, but separate from, *how much* you are able to
earn and how closely you maintain the same level
of financial compensation for your labors after the
accident. If you are a musician and crush your hand
in an automobile accident, you most likely will need
to discontinue playing the piano for a living. However, you may be able to receive re-training and
begin a new profession as a real estate agent.

*Different injuries produce different results for
different people,* and you and your medical team
will discover as you recover from your injury
what, if any, limitations you'll be facing in the
future.

In this case, you will need to prove that the pain
and suffering of being forced to leave your beloved
profession, *even if the change resulted in an increased income for you*, demands financial
reimbursement. Your ability to succeed on these
complex issues is directly related to your ability to
successfully negotiate everything the insurance in-

dustry will throw in your way to make it look like you may be *better off* financially after losing your hand.

More typical are those cases where injuries received in an automobile accident either temporarily or permanently, and partially or substantially, limit your ability to perform the work that you did before the accident. A back injury can limit you to lifting no more than five pounds, when before the accident you were hefting 80-pound packing boxes with ease. Cervical trauma can prohibit you from sitting for more than 20 minutes at your computer, where before your injury you worked four- and five-hour stretches without a break.

The most critical aspect of documenting how your injury affects your ability to perform your job is the medical record created by your treating physician. Your doctor isn't going to be able to record your limitations in the chart unless you *clearly and consistently communicate those limitations during each medical examination.*

*If your doctor orders you to permanently limit, restrict, or change your employment, the calculation of anticipated wage loss becomes extraordinarily complex. You should hire a qualified personal injury attorney to represent you and negotiate a settlement that will protect you and your family from a lifetime of financial loss.*

**If at any time your employment conditions change, whether it's short-term or long-term, notify the insurance company *immediately* so that they are prepared to respond to your eventual claims for related wage loss.**

If your condition improves, let your doctor know that your ability to conduct your work is also improving. However, if your injury continues to prohibit you from doing your work, you have two choices: either change your treatment plan to provide more successful treatment of the injury, or change your working environment. Your treating physician is most knowledgeable about the appropriate course of action for you.

If your doctor orders you to change your working environment, you will need to involve your employer. Legal requirements prohibit discrimination against disabled workers. Your employer will likely respond quickly to a physician's orders to accommodate special needs required by the nature of your injury, especially if those special needs are short-term. Special needs may mean a five minute break every hour to alleviate stresses on your neck, or re-assignment to a job that doesn't require lifting heavy loads.

Complications arise if your doctor's orders require substantial accommodations or long-term special considerations. There are some instances where an employer simply won't be able to meet your special needs. If, for example, you are a carpenter working in a small cabinet shop, and you lose the ability to use your right arm, there may not be alternative employment opportunities at that particular business that reasonably match your reduced abilities.

In this case, your doctor will order alternative vocational training that allows you to perform work that is better-suited to your diminished physical abilities.

## Quality of Work Checklist

If your doctor has ordered you not to return to your previous job or has ordered you to permanently reduce or restrict employment, provide testimony and medical records documenting this. Documentation should include:

❑ Date of accident.

❑ Date employment limitations began.

❑ Anticipated date of return to employment.

❑ Why you are unable to work, detailing specific injuries that contribute.

❑ Any restrictions against returning to your former employment.

❑ Specifics about the temporary or permanent nature of your disability.

❑ If applicable, your physician's orders to retrain or seek alternate employment.

❑ A detailed list of those functions of your job that you are unable to perform as a result of the accident. Provide medical records supporting your claims. Some functional losses may include an inability to: get to work, lift, sit, stand, bend, cradle the telephone, drive, operate a computer, operate machinery or heavy equipment, stock, reach overhead, carry a sample case or other required equipment, wear required uniform or safety equipment, use common tools, or perform typical office tasks (like stapling, collating, photocopying or filing).

*Determining future wage loss is a process of applying complex mathematical formulas to established industry norms and statistics. If you find yourself in a situation where you are forced to change your vocation or stop working altogether, you absolutely must have representation by an attorney trained in this complex area of the law.*

❏ Documentation of the limitations caused by injuries that may not be related to physical movement, such as: memory loss; speech, sight or other sensory impairments; disfigurement or other disability that affects your ability to deal with the public; restrictions because of prescribed medication; level of energy; or depression-related disabilities.

❏ A detailed list of any work-related functions and activities in which you were unable to participate as a result of the accident, such as the annual retreat, continuing education, business seminars, or business promotions. Detail how your financial compensation was impacted.

## Documenting How Your Injury Affects Your Quality of Life

It is just as important to document the effects of the injury on your *personal* life as it is to document how the accident affected your ability to work and earn a living. In fact, many accident victims find that it is in basic day-to-day living that they experience the most severe problems and difficulties as they recover from their injuries.

The best way to document how the accident has negatively impacted the quality of your life is to think about everything you do from the time you wake up until you go to sleep. Consider also all of the things you do (or used to do) outside of your home, whether taking care of personal business or pursuing your favorite hobbies.

174

Here is a sample checklist that may help you to identify and document the many areas of your life that can be adversely affected by an injury.

## Quality of Life Checklist

❏ Are there any limitations when you bathe, groom, or dress yourself?

Difficulty getting in and out of the bathtub; holding the hair dryer over your head causes numbness in the arm; inability to lean over and pull on hosiery because of back spasms; your dentures don't fit because the required medication dehydrated your mouth; you can't wear high heels due to low back pain.

❏ Has your ability to prepare meals been affected?

You can't lift dishes from overhead shelves; standing for long periods at the stove causes severe leg pains; the rotating motion of stirring ingredients causes wrist pain; loss of appetite prevents any joy of cooking.

❏ Is your ability to maintain the household limited?

Can't push the vacuum cleaner; unable to bend over to pick up children's toys; knee injury precludes kneeling to clean the floors; continuing back pain prevents taking the dog for morning walk; stiffness in your hands make doing dishes impossible; unable to maintain garden because of limited mobility.

❏ Are you able to manage your customary daily business errands and activities?

Can't carry the shopping basket because of tenderness in elbow; inability to load/unload groceries from the car because of back spasms; inability to stand in line at Post Office because of swelling in injured ankles.

❏ Are you able to transport yourself with the same degree of ease and comfort?

Unable to drive without abject terror; opening the heavy car door causes pain in shoulder; your doctor told you not to ride a bicycle until you get knee replacement surgery; unable to turn neck to check for traffic; trips longer than ten minutes cause extreme lower back pain; you can't take the bus anymore because you can't stand longer than five minutes; can't lift the baby out of the car seat.

❏ Are you and your partner or family experiencing problems?

You haven't been able to go camping all summer because of headaches; you haven't been able to have sex in eight months because of the back surgery; you quit drinking for 14 years, but started again right after the accident because your pain was so intense; your kids are afraid to ask you to do anything because you always burst into tears; your husband left and filed for divorce

*Personal injury attorneys typically use a combination of effective methods to document the effects of an injury on the quality of life. Written and audio testimonies, photographs, videotapes, and high-tech computerized graphics and narratives are often used to provide compelling proof of disability.*

because he said you're impossible to live with since the accident; you gained 65 pounds and your wife refuses to go anywhere with you; ever since you went on anti-depressant medication, you don't have the energy to do anything with your husband.

❏ Are you having difficulties with your social relationships?

You had to resign from the Board of Directors because you just don't have the energy to perform the tasks; your bridge group won't come to your house anymore because you can't clean the house; you haven't been asked out once since you started using the cane; ever since you had to quit working, you never see your friends from work; you've gained 25 pounds and you're just too depressed to visit your friends; all your friends are into wind surfing and since the accident you never see them anymore.

❏ Are you experiencing financial problems because of the accident?

You can't do the housework any more so now you have to pay $240 a month to a maid service; you couldn't plant your vegetable garden this year and now you're spending $150 more each month for produce at the grocery store; you had to cancel your family's health club membership because you can't afford it; you sold the car to buy groceries; you haven't worked for six months; the bank foreclosed on the house and you're in collections with all your creditors; you postponed getting braces for your son because you couldn't work and lost your dental coverage.

❏ Have you noticed a personality change?

You used to have a great sense of humor, but nothing makes you laugh any more; you're so frustrated by these new physical limitations, you just cry all the time; your whole life seems like one big doctor's appointment; after 30 years in the business, now they tell you that you have to change jobs, and it scares you to death; you never felt that anything could stop you from working out and feeling healthy and strong, and now you feel like a disabled, nervous wreck; all these medications make you feel weird all day long; you used to love being around children, but you just can't handle their physical demands any more; the chronic pain makes you feel angry all the time.

❏ Are you able to enjoy the "fun" things you used to enjoy?

You can't play the piano because suspending your arms causes severe back spasms; you gave up bowling because of migraines; you can't ski because of the cervical fusion; you gave up coaching Little League because you can't manage the equipment; you lost your

recreational pilot's license because of
required medications; because of your back
injury, this is the first year in 30 years that
you haven't planted your flower garden; you
can't lift your 5-year-old son and he keeps
asking why you don't play with him any
more; you had to sell your horse because
your doctor told you never to ride again.

❏ Are you having trouble sleeping?
You're always exhausted because you can't
get any sleep; you sleep too much and sleep
right through the alarm; you're up every two
hours with back and neck pain; you're
having terrible nightmares about the collision; you had to buy a new adjustable bed
just so you could sleep.

Of course, your own lifestyle, habits, and hobbies
will dictate your personal list of how the accident
injuries have affected the quality of your life. The
important thing to remember is that when it comes
time to prove pain, suffering, and financial losses,
the insurance company will want verifiable, documented proof that your life changed significantly
after the accident, and that those changes were directly related to the accident.

When evaluating how the injury diminished the
quality of your life, the most important allies on
your documentation team are your physician and
your family, friends, and associates. Your physician is especially important because the effects of
the injury that you mention to your doctor are re-

corded in your medical charts and become a valuable part of the documentation trail leading to successful settlement.

Your family is a vital source of information and documentation of the debilitating effects of the accident. They are the people who see first-hand how you may have been forced to adjust your life to meet the demands and limitations of your injury and recovery. As you prepare for settlement negotiations, you will want to obtain written or recorded statements from your family that substantiate and validate your claims of pain, suffering, and financial loss.

## Summary

A fundamental part of negotiating a successful settlement is providing the documentation that supports your claim. In this chapter, we talked about how automobile accident injuries can limit your physical, emotional, and mental abilities. These impairments can adversely affect your job, your personal life, and the financial future of you and your family.

Being injured in an automobile accident is a very serious and traumatic event. Those people who choose to walk away from such an experience without pursuing treatment or negotiating financial compensation for their losses may be making a mistake that will haunt them physically, emotionally, and financially for the rest of their lives.

If you are suffering in any way because of your automobile accident, you first need to do everything in your power to seek appropriate medical treatment. You also need to actively pursue compensation for your ordeal. If you don't think you can do any of these things on your own, ask for help. Your family, friends, employer, doctor, and your attorney can be valuable members of your team if only you *communicate your needs.*

We can guide you to appropriate health care and we can direct your attention to documenting those areas where you have experienced the greatest losses. We can even recommend when to seek professional legal help. But in the end, you alone will make the decisions that will ultimately dictate the success or failure of your recovery on all fronts.

If you have been injured in an automobile accident, there is no reason for you to assume or expect that your damages and losses are yours to bear indefinitely without remedy or relief. The law is on your side, but the responsibility for seeing that it remains there is yours alone.

Remember that you have the right to be compensated for your pain, suffering, and financial losses. Provide the necessary facts to the insurance company with organized, detailed documentation; skillfully negotiate the terms; and confidently demand what is rightfully and reasonably yours.

## Survival Guide Checklist

☐ If you need help dealing with your automobile accident, don't be afraid to ask for it!

☐ Both physical and emotional injuries require immediate treatment.

☐ Document everything as it occurs to make your claim more manageable at settlement time.

☐ Ask your employer for help when documenting the impact of the accident on your ability to work.

☐ Be aware of the effects of the accident on your personal life.

**NOTES**

# The Art of Settling Your Claim

Throughout this book we've talked about the importance of keeping track of everything related to your accident, injuries, and medical treatment. All of your notes, records, reports, and bills need to be collected, reviewed, and consolidated in a package that will prove your claim for damages.

Gathering and organizing, or *marshaling*, your medical reports and bills is by far the most important component of your settlement demand package. In this chapter, we'll give you some helpful guidelines on how to most efficiently collect and present these materials to the insurance company. Later in this chapter, we're going to talk briefly about how to prepare and present your settlement demand letter.

## Marshaling Records and Bills

Starting from day one, you'll need to collect all of the medical records and bills from all of the medical providers who have treated your injuries. You'll also need to keep track of all other medical care that you received during this time, even if it doesn't directly relate to your accident injuries.

If the insurance company discovers that you have withheld information about receiving medical care of any kind since the accident, they may be able to successfully claim that you purposefully withheld information. They may claim that other injuries or illnesses had an adverse effect on your recovery from the accident injuries and are not the insured driver's fault.

What may appear to you to be unrelated medical care could actually be related to your accident injuries. It's important to gather all of your medical records and thoroughly review them to see if any of your seemingly unrelated medical treatment may in fact be related to your accident. For example, problems with your dental alignment that mysteriously show up after a rear-end collision may be related to a TMJ condition contributed to by cervical sprain suffered in the accident.

Take the time to list all of your care providers. They might include an ambulance company, hospital emergency room, physical therapist, dentist, Chiropractor, massage therapist, orthopedist, and X-ray technician. Hospitals often contract out to independent medical companies for diagnostic and testing procedures. Your hospital bill may reflect only partial charges. Other services may be billed to you separately. Ask lots of questions of each billing office.

These types of bills and records often become lost in the shuffle, especially if some time has passed between the accident and the commencement of settlement negotiations. Also, if your insurance is billed directly for your medical care, you may not actually see many of the bills. You will need to personally contact each provider and request an itemized statement for all services provided.

When requesting your records from a care provider, be sure to request the entire file. If you submit just a general request for medical records, the care provider will sometimes send only what they think you may need. The entire file might include notes, correspondence between the provider and the insurance company, and miscellaneous test reports that are vitally important to your case.

You'll have to pay for copies of the entire file, so it's important that you work out payment details with the care providers when you're requesting the records. Washington law sets the standard fees that medical practitioners can charge for records. You should familiarize yourself with those fees.

You may also request copies of your medical bills from your own health insurance carrier. There is customarily no charge for this service, but you need to request the bills in writing. When writing your request, make sure you are precise about which bills you are requesting, and for what period of time.

Apart from your medical records and bills, you should also request written narrative reports from

*Professional personal injury attorneys are adept at identifying, requesting, and systematically organizing the comprehensive records, bills and reports that are generated following injury in an automobile accident.*

your caregivers. These reports should verify the nature and extent of your injuries, the required care, your lifestyle changes, and the likelihood of permanency and future treatment. Ask the provider's office for the cost of a report. Doctors' report charges vary, but most will require that you pay in advance. It's sometimes no easy task to convince a busy medical practitioner to take the time to prepare a written report for you, but persistence and a thoughtful *pre*payment for the doctor's report will usually produce results.

If you are unable to handle document management of this scope, or are if you can't afford the cost of requesting records and reports, you may want to refer the task to an attorney. Law office staff and resources are geared to extensive document management, and the costs of securing the documents are typically advanced by the attorney and deducted from the final settlement amount. This spares you the hardship of large out-of-pocket expenses during your negotiations.

When you have all of your records, review them to make sure that you have an accurate, comprehensive chronology of your care. If any records or bills are missing, request them from the appropriate provider. The insurance company will review your history of care very thoroughly, and you must have the same information they do if you're to launch successful settlement negotiations.

Set up a system that works for you. Organize all of the records and bills by provider in chronological order. If you have not already done so, provide a copy of each document to the insurance company. Make sure that you also keep a copy of everything for your own records. It's not unusual to forward documents to the insurance company only to be told months down the line that they were never received or were misplaced and have to be replaced.

The records and bills that you gather from all of your health care providers will provide the substance of your settlement demand package. Taking the time now as you receive them to document and organize what can turn out to be hundreds of pages of records and bills will make for more efficient and effective preparation of your settlement demand later.

## Determining the Value of Your Case

In Chapter 7, we talked about the many different ways an injury can affect the quality of your life, both vocationally and avocationally. Once you have identified all of the different ways in which the accident has impacted your life, you will need to take a second look and determine the *value* of those losses.

When you ask the insurance company for a settlement that fairly compensates you for your losses, you will need to present a relatively accurate idea of the worth of the losses. You will need to specify the financial losses and how the injuries damaged your quality of life.

The determination of value rests in large part on the actual injuries suffered in the accident. Insurance adjusters do not have an industry rule book to find out how much they should pay for an injury. Based on their years of experience and company resources, they generally have a pretty good feel for a reasonable settlement amount for a particular injury or injuries. If you are trying to settle your own case, you are at a distinct disadvantage. You don't have years of experience and voluminous statistics upon which to base a reasonable value for your claim. If you are uncertain about what is a reasonable claim value, don't hesitate to consult with a personal injury attorney who may be able to provide you with some ballpark figures.

There is no set formula or rule by which you can make a determination of loss and value. This is very difficult to do. Experts in insurance and law spend years developing the ability to evaluate cases and come up with a consistent range of value for each case.

Your claim value depends on a combination of many things. Foremost in any claim valuation is the extent and severity of your injuries. If your injuries are permanent and disabling in nature, then your claim value increases. Provided, of course, that your care providers thoroughly document your claim. In addition to the injuries themselves, you also need to consider how those injuries affected the quality of your life and your lifestyle. The insurance company will require extensive documentation from you to prove your claim that the injury curtailed your ability to live your life as you did before the accident.

The insurance company will also take into consideration other, less objective facts when reviewing your claim. They'll be looking for characteristics of your claim that will assist them in assigning your claim a value on the low end of the settlement range.

*Determining future losses caused by disabling injury is a difficult procedure. If you have permanently disabling injuries, you must have an experienced personal injury attorney represent you against the insurance company.*

What are the indicators that alert the insurance company to a lower claim value? For starters, a lack of corroborating statements from your medical care providers will immediately diminish the value of your claim. Also, if you are untruthful or inconsistent in your statements, the insurance company will focus on that and greatly reduce or entirely reject your claim.

Other alarms that encourage an insurance company to fight your claim are the existence of prior injuries, especially those that you failed to disclose to the insurance company early in your negotiations with them.

How you pursued and obtained medical treatment for your injuries is crucial in setting the value of your claim. If you did not see a doctor for treatment until long after you were originally injured, the insurance company will rightfully suspect that your injuries may not have been all that serious because they didn't warrant immediate medical attention. Gaps in your medical care are also bad news for your claim's value. If you discontinued treatment three months after the accident, and then resumed treatment seven months later, the insurance company is going to decide that your lack of need for any medical care during that long period indicates that you recovered from your injuries early on. The insurance company is not going to be very responsive to your claims that many months after the accident, you've suddenly discovered that you now need medical care.

Many years of experience and statistics prove that certain injuries require certain medical care. If your medical care departs from the established standard of care, the insurance company is going to quickly suspect that you are not receiving necessary or reasonable care and they will in turn reject your claim.

Another reason for a low valuation or outright rejection of your claim is if you see only one provider and submit excessive medical bills, especially if you failed to obtain any relief or improvement for your injuries. A common misconception among the general public is that an insurance settlement should somehow equal three times the medical bills. This is not true. As much as we may not want to believe it, specific injuries dictate specific settlement amounts. If your specific injuries are only valued at $10,000, the insurance company is not going to provide a higher settlement amount if you pursue excessive medical care that rings up a bill of $15,000.

The insurance company will pay a settlement that fairly compensates you for your damages and losses. If you accumulate medical costs that do not accurately reflect typical care for the types of injuries that you received, the insurance company is under no obligation whatsoever to compensate you for the excessive medical charges, unless your providers clearly document the need for extraordinary care.

## Negotiation Strategies

When evaluating your claim for settlement, the insurance adjuster also considers you as an individual, apart from your actual injuries. It's important to meet personally with the adjuster early in your negotiations. A face-to-face meeting provides you with an opportunity to get to know the adjuster. It also gives the adjuster an opportunity to assess your likability. This is important!

If your case fails to settle and makes its way into a courtroom, the jury is going to make a determination of financial compensation based in large part on how much they like you as a person. The adjuster knows this all too well. When you make a good first impression, the adjuster will remember this and make every attempt to fairly settle your case without having to take it to trial.

What makes a good impression? Your physical appearance counts for a lot. Good grooming, appropriate attire, and confident body language spells "I'm a likable person!" to the adjuster. A clear speaking manner, friendliness, and fairness, plus a good understanding of the facts of your case, puts *you* in control and sets the tone for future negotiations.

> Gaining control early on and keeping that control is what will make or break your claim for a settlement. Confidence, clear communication, and a good physical impression put control in your corner early on. Persistence, consistency, and accurate and complete documentation keeps it there throughout your negotiations.

You'll want to display a willingness to discuss your settlement openly, fairly, and without resorting to argument, threats or abusive language. There's a big difference between being intelligently assertive and belligerently aggressive. The adjuster is not going to be very responsive to your demands for a high value if you jump all over him and make unreasonable demands in an argumentative, in-your-face fashion.

If you make a bad first impression, the adjuster is going to realize early on that you are not likely to pose a risk of a higher settlement at trial. You can quickly make a bad impression if you appear poorly groomed or inappropriately dressed for a business meeting. You're doomed if you don't have all the facts about your case straight. If you appear disorganized, disinterested, or uninformed, the adjuster is going to take this as an open invitation to control the outcome of your settlement right from the beginning.

The first time the adjuster catches you misrepresenting the facts of your case, you've immediately blown any chance of an equitable settlement. *Be honest.* If you don't know the answer to a question asked by the adjuster, say so. Don't try to guess or make up something that you think will help your case.

When it comes time to actively negotiate your settlement, there are a variety of strategies. Some experts believe that it's important to start high, then work down from there. Others claim that the best strategy is to determine the settlement amount you want, start with that number, and *stick to it.*

---

**The best strategy is the one that you feel comfortable using, and that fits with the personality, professional habits, and experience of the insurance adjuster.**

---

Try to get a feel early on of where the adjuster stands on negotiation strategies. If the adjuster begins your first discussion with "We'll give you $10,000, and not a penny more" and hangs up the phone, you may not have much room to negotiate. However, most adjusters are instructed by their employers to provide a settlement that rests somewhere on the low end of reasonable. This means that there is actually quite a bit of room to negotiate. Many insurance adjusters are in the business because they *enjoy* negotiating, and the ones who have been in the business for a while are darn good at it.

What's the trick to successful negotiations? It depends on what's being negotiated, who is doing the negotiations, and the environment in which the negotiations are taking place.

Smaller dollar amounts shouldn't require excessive negotiations. If you're squabbling into the third week with the insurance adjuster over your demand for $4,000 and the insurance company's settlement offer is $3,750, and nobody's giving an inch, there's something wrong with this picture. Is it really worth your time, effort, and emotional well-being to drag out a difference of only $250? At some point, pride has to give way to reason. In this case, you would probably be better off taking the $3,750 and putting the settlement negotiations behind you.

Conversely, larger dollar amounts customarily involve more extensive negotiations. If you're claiming $75,000 in medical costs, pain, and suffering, the insurance adjuster is obligated to define a settlement that best represents the interests of the insurance company (keeping money in their bank account) while maintaining a good faith effort to provide a reasonable settlement to you (paying you an amount that fairly represents compensation for your losses). In situations where the injured party's demand is in the tens of thousands of dollars, it is not unusual to see a similar difference — tens of thousands of dollars — between your demand and the insurance company's offer early in the negotiations.

In every situation requiring negotiation, and especially where negotiations will likely continue for a period of time, there are a few basic negotiation strategies to remember.

First, remember that your negotiating strategy is not just a matter of figuring out how much your case is worth. More importantly, you need to figure out how you are going to *prove* the reasonableness of your claim and maximize its amount. *Any claim is only as good as its proof.* Marshal your records and bills, provide ample supporting documentation, provide statements from family, friends and co-workers, and communicate your own personal experiences clearly and consistently. These negotiation strategies will go a long way toward establishing proof of your claim.

Try to get a good understanding of how much your case is worth. If you choose to do this on your own without the assistance of a professional, you'll need to do some research at a local law library. Review the settlement amounts of cases that have gone to trial, and identify those cases where the injuries closely match yours. Talk to people you know who were similarly injured and received recent insurance settlements.

Know what you're going to ask for, and what you're actually going to settle for. These two amounts may be significantly different. The important thing is that you decide early on what your bottom dollar is, and stick to it. The insurance adjuster will sense that you're serious about your settlement claim, and will more than likely respond with reasonable counter-offers to your demands.

Of course, if you provide a figure early on and the insurance adjuster immediately agrees and rushes the settlement papers to your house in thirty minutes or less, that's a clue that you probably just sold yourself short. What can you do in this case? Probably nothing. Once you give control of the negotiations to the insurance company by agreeing to a particular settlement amount, there's not much you can do to convince them to bring it higher.

**Get to know the adjuster personally. Conduct the negotiations on the adjuster's territory. Everyone is more likely to give concessions and cut a little more slack if they're feeling comfortable and dominant on their own turf.**

Be persistent! A phone call each day is not excessive. "Just calling to see if you've had a chance to review my recent settlement demand." "Wanted to touch base with you to see if there's anything you needed to help you make a decision on my settlement claim." Offering to do something for the adjuster in exchange for a concession by him is an effective strategy. Ask the adjustor, "What do *you* need that will make it easier for you to come up to $7,000?" If you make such an offer to make the adjuster's job easier, follow through immediately!

Negotiating a settlement claim is just like buying a car or a house. The experts all agree that your best strategy is to take all of your emotional involvement out of the negotiations. This is difficult to do when you're trying to settle your own case, especially when you're asking for compensation for your personal pain and suffering. Keep it factual, make it informational, and remain as objective as you possibly can.

Listen! The most successful negotiators learn to listen to the other party. If you're busy talking, you can't hear what the insurance adjuster has to say about your claim. If the adjuster voices a concern about some element of your claim, focus your attention on the adjuster's objection and put your energies into identifying a solution that will overcome the objection. A good response might be, "What can I do to make that more acceptable to you?" Then LISTEN to the adjuster's suggestion, and take appropriate ACTION.

Negotiation is not a win or lose situation. It's a *compromise*. Threats, anger, or accusations will not work to your advantage when you're negotiating with the insurance company. Being overly reactive, argumentative, pushy, or unreasonably stubborn will offend the adjuster and turn the negotiations

*A personal injury professional can calculate future losses for wages, retirement and other benefits. These calculations require technical expertise.*

into a one-sided and possibly personalized battle where the adjuster will simply turn you off and refuse to budge an inch.

On the other hand, if you truly feel that the adjuster is not responding fairly or responsibly to your *reasonable* demands, don't hesitate to go above the adjuster and voice your concern about the handling of your case to the supervisor. But do so calmly and intelligently. Screaming at the adjuster's supervisor will only accomplish the result of encouraging *two* employees of the insurance company to do everything in their power to thwart your efforts to obtain a reasonable settlement.

If you find that your settlement negotiations are deadlocked, and nobody's moving in either direction, it's time to take a close look and determine what's not working. What are you or the adjuster doing that is stalling the negotiations? Sit down with the adjuster and talk frankly about the situation. Ask the adjuster for suggestions on how to bridge the gap. This is something that most people find hard to do. However, if you keep a cool head and focus on the importance of compromise rather than winning all the chips, you may find a successful resolution to the stalemate.

The best settlement will result from negotiations during which you become the adjuster's working partner. Whatever you can do to make the adjuster's job easier and his or her life more pleasant will probably be rewarded by more cooperative and conciliatory responses from the adjuster. This is not to say that you have to beg or bribe the adjuster into reaching a reasonable settlement.

If your claim is reasonable, and backed up by comprehensive documentation that lends the required proof to your claim, then your cooperative and proactive approach to the adjuster's handling of your claim will be successful. You'll be able to overcome the standard objections and hesitations that any insurance adjuster must, by his or her job definition, apply to your claim and the final settlement value. Both of you will walk away from the negotiation table knowing that reason and fairness prevailed. And that's a successful closure to any settlement negotiation.

## Presenting an Effective Demand Package

Once you have achieved maximum medical improvement, it's time to gather your documentation and other resources and prepare an effective demand package.

The demand package is the actual document and other supporting material that is provided to the insurance company. It's the official demand for settlement of your case. Typically, you want to include some standard components in your demand package.

**Theme**. This is usually a short paragraph that introduces the demand package. The theme sells your case to the insurance company. It personalizes your experience, and portrays you as a likable person living a good life until tragedy struck.

A sample theme might be:

*This is a 26-year-old woman who spent the past twenty years of her life preparing for a career in ballet. Since the accident, she has been unable to dance and has been forced to give up her life's dream of becoming a professional dancer, discontinue training with world-renowned performing artists, move out of her apartment on Broadway in New York City, and start a struggling career as a real estate sales agent in Tukwila while living with her elderly parents.*

The theme of your demand package grabs the reader's attention and provides a real, human perspective to the damage and loss caused by the accident.

**Accident Summary.** This section summarizes the facts of the accident, including date, time, location, and participants. A description of how the accident occurred should include the resulting property damage and any law enforcement action.

**Injuries and Medical Treatment.** Describe the nature and extent of your injuries, including required medical treatment. When discussing medical treatment, special attention is given to addressing the need for that care and the reasonableness of the charges. The degree of temporary impairment and the degree of permanent impairment should be clearly stated, with discussion of the implications that occur because of any permanent injury. This is where you would refer to the theme, discussing how the injuries adversely affected the quality of your vocational and avocational life.

Most everyone's self esteem is guided by what they do. If you can't do what you love to do because of the accident, you have suffered a traumatic loss. Identify the loss and develop your narrative around that theme.

Include a chart in your demand letter that (1) separately summarizes all of the medical bills and providers, (2) provides subtotals for each provider, and (3) provides a grand total for all medical care.

**Expenses**. Provide a narrative detailing all of your out-of-pocket expenses, including mileage to and from your health care providers. A table displaying itemized expenses and a grand total is an effective method for communicating this information.

**Future Losses.** Any future economic losses should also be included and summarized in a table. Include future medical bills, wage loss, and out-of-pocket expenses. Your medical provider should be able to provide some indication of anticipated future medical costs.

**Demand Summary.** Wrap up your demand letter with a brief summary of the most important points of your claim. Be sure to refer to your theme. Provide the dollar amount of your claim, and provide a time frame within which you expect a response.

## Producing Your Demand Package

Insurance companies are accustomed to receiving professionally prepared demand packages from attorneys. You may not have the resources to produce a top-notch package with supporting computer-generated graphics and a professionally produced video documentary. You can take certain steps, however, to ensure that your demand package will be noticed and thoroughly reviewed by the insurance company.

### Demand Package Checklist

❏ Provide a sturdy cover. Any stationery or office supply store sells a wide variety of report covers. Make sure the pages of your demand letter are securely fastened to the cover.

❏ Separate the sections of your demand letter. You can use tab inserts, or you can simply insert a colored piece of paper between the sections and write the appropriate section title on the colored insert.

❏ Type the demand letter. Handwritten demand letters will not be taken seriously by the insurance company, and may be difficult or impossible to read.

❏ Include photographs, diagrams, drawings, and videotapes if you have them. Any visual media that supports your demand are acceptable. A color photo effectively displaying your injuries may be enlarged at a photocopy service and affixed to the cover of your demand letters. This virtually guarantees that you'll grab the adjuster's attention.

❏ Attach all relevant records, bills, reports, letters, and testimonials. Provide a summary index page that lists all of the attachments.

❏ Prepare a copy of the demand package for your files. Reference it as you continue to negotiate your settlement demand with the insurance company.

## Summary

The most important aspect of successful settlement negotiations is *preparation*. Preparation means arming yourself with the tools and skills that you need to persuade the insurance company to provide a settlement that is reasonable and fair. Preparation also means managing your bills, records, reports, and other supporting documentation in a manner that establishes indisputable proof of your injuries and your claim for compensation.

Most folks find that they can manage just about everything that's required for successful settlement, right up until they hit the documentation wall. It requires certain administrative and organizational skills, and no small amount of time, energy, and effort, to effectively marshal all of your documentation resources. Making a commitment to successful settlement negotiations also means making a substantial commitment to the drudgery and frustration of managing the document trail that leads from your accident to settlement negotiations.

People simply aren't *born* with successful negotiation skills. These skills are *learned* through trial and error. As you embark on your settlement negotiations, the simple negotiating guidelines that we've provided in this chapter should help you stay on track and remain focused on your settlement goal.

Remember, negotiation is a compromise. It's the gray area between what you want, and what the insurance company wants. Believe it or not, negotiation can even be *fun* if you've got the right frame of mind. If you approach negotiation as a black and white battle of win or lose or right or wrong, no matter how much you come away with in settlement, you're likely to walk away from a bad experience.

Everything gets resolved, one way or the other. Your job when negotiating your own insurance settlement is deciding what you want, how you're going to get it, and working *with* the insurance adjuster to reach your objectives.

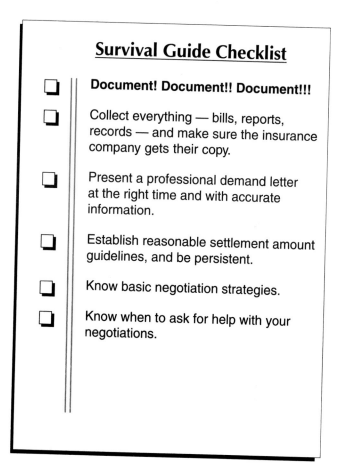

## <u>Survival Guide Checklist</u>

☐ **Document! Document!! Document!!!**

☐ Collect everything — bills, reports, records — and make sure the insurance company gets their copy.

☐ Present a professional demand letter at the right time and with accurate information.

☐ Establish reasonable settlement amount guidelines, and be persistent.

☐ Know basic negotiation strategies.

☐ Know when to ask for help with your negotiations.

# Graham Crackers

"Fortunately Mr. Ozaki's insurance company made no distinction between an Act of God and an Act of Godzilla."

# Settlement Options

We've shared the many different tools and skills you will need to successfully settle your insurance claim in previous chapters. Put your best effort into applying those tools and take full advantage of your time, temperament, and talent to generate a successful and reasonable insurance settlement.

But what happens when settlement negotiations fail? The insurance company is bound by law to make a diligent attempt at a fair settlement. You are equally bound to pursue your settlement negotiations in a reasonable and ethical manner. Sometimes, though, parties find themselves in situations where a fair, timely settlement just simply doesn't seem possible. In these situations, you may find yourself pulling your hair out by the handfuls and pounding your fist on the telephone. But there are alternatives!

## Settlement Alternatives

There are several things you can do if your own settlement negotiations are failing.

1. **Give up, walk away, and never look back.** A lousy option, and one that we don't recommend. But it *is* an alternative nonetheless. Choosing this option means that the insurance company wins, and you lose. You may regret it the rest of your life, especially if your damages and injuries continue to reduce the quality of your life. Remember that the insurance industry *thrives* on people who choose this option, then stumble away to a lifetime of physical pain and financial misery without compensation.

2. **Cave in early to the insurance company's demands.** A truly unappetizing option that sometimes looks like the only way to achieve closure on your claim. However, before accepting an offer that you are clearly not happy with, consult an attorney to make sure you're *not* giving away the barn when you could have walked away with the whole farm. Free consultation may disclose a flaw in your strategy that might damage the outcome of your negotiations.

3. **Consult an attorney.** A very good option, especially when you've already applied everything you've learned in this book

and are still getting nowhere fast. AL-
WAYS keep this option open, *especially if
you find that the stress of settlement
negotiations is slowing your physical
recovery.*

4. **Arbitrate**. An excellent idea! Read more
   about this popular method of dispute
   resolution below.

5. **Mediate**. Another excellent idea! We'll
   talk more about mediation later in this
   chapter.

6. **Hold out for litigation.** Rarely a good
   idea. Read on for the reasons why.

## Arbitration

Arbitration is a dispute resolution method that has
grown increasingly popular as court calendars sag
under the weight of two- and three-year delays and
escalating trial costs. Arbitration is a quick and efficient way to resolve your claim without the costs,
time delays, and exhaustive hassles of courtroom
litigation.

Many public and private groups offer arbitration
services to claimants at reasonable cost. (The Yellow Pages will provide a listing of the arbitration
services in your area.) Your insurance company may
also be able to suggest an arbitration service that
they have used in the past.

When you agree to go into arbitration, you participate in the selection of the arbitrator. A professional

arbitrator generally has extensive experience in the law. An arbitrator may be a retired judge or a practicing attorney. The arbitrator will listen to your side of the case, and will also listen to the insurance company's side in an informal, relaxed setting. The arbitrator will conduct discussions with both parties to gain an understanding of the issues and circumstances of the case. It is the arbitrator's job to act as an objective, unbiased intermediary during these discussions.

After extensive interviews and discussions with the parties, the arbitrator will close the meeting and independently review and evaluate the merits of the case. He or she will then determine a settlement amount.

An arbitrator will often grant an award that falls somewhere between the insurance company's most recent offer and your most recent demand. Arbitration is not the environment where large, dramatic sums are awarded. (Nor are jury trials, despite common belief.) This is not an environment where you are likely to walk away with nothing. It's a professionally structured, non-threatening environment that may be the best place to resolve stalled negotiations.

Arbitration is similar to a trial in that all of the facts of the case are presented to the arbitrator who then acts as "judge" and "jury" and decides the outcome of the case. The big differences are that arbitration (1) is far less costly, (2) requires much less preparation, (3) is far more expedient, and (4) produces substantially less stress than a trial.

Arbitration typically costs about $1,500, and is nearly always less risky and less stressful than courtroom litigation. Many insurance companies are responsive to a demand for arbitration, because it means lower legal costs to them.

---

If you find that your settlement negotiations aren't getting anywhere, and especially if the insurance company's offer is significantly lower than your demand, you may want to consider arbitration. This is an excellent environment for neutral and reasoned discussion and resolution of your respective claims.

---

When the parties involved in a dispute undertake to arbitrate a matter, they agree beforehand if the arbitrator's final decision will be *binding* or *non-binding*. If the decision is binding, the participants in the arbitration may not petition the court to change the decision after the proceedings have concluded. However, if the decision is not binding, the parties involved may turn to the courts if they are dissatisfied with the outcome of arbitration.

## Mediation

Mediation is an alternative to arbitration, and is growing in popularity as parties sitting on opposite sides of a dispute discover this low-cost solution to their conflicts. A typical mediation will cost under

213

$1,000, and the bill is shared equally by the parties to the mediation.

Mediation is not based on the relative *merits* of the case. This means that you will not be going into the details of your case with the mediator (nor will the insurance company). In mediation, it's assumed that all of the history of the case has already been discussed and understood by the parties. The facts, claims, or beliefs of the parties are not relevant during mediation. The mediator is primarily concerned with bringing the respective parties to a point of agreement on the dollar amount of the settlement. Mediation is a streamlined exercise by the mediator to bring the parties to a financial resolution.

The mediator will ask the insurance company for its highest possible settlement offer, and will ask you for the lowest dollar amount that you would be willing to accept. Without disclosing the other party's "bottom line," the mediator then proceeds to work with both parties to discover what it will take to bring the parties to a common figure.

Example: You're asking for $20,000 compensation for your injuries, pain, and suffering. You refuse to take any less, because you're still going to your Chiropractor for pain relief and you're concerned that your medical care will continue beyond any settlement date. The insurance company solidly refuses to offer more than $12,000, because your medical care to date totals $5,400 and they really don't think you'll need additional medical care. The two of you have been going around around for months on these figures, but are hopelessly stalled.

The mediator will note the respective dollar amounts and begin discussions with both sides to reach a compromise. The mediator may be able to get the insurance company to come up to $14,000, and provide a guarantee that they'll pick up whatever reasonable and related medical costs you incur over the next three years. This is an acceptable compromise to you and the insurance company. It calms your fears about future medical costs and puts cash in your pocket now.

The insurance company is happy because it doesn't have to pony up much more cash than it was willing to pay coming into mediation. It allows the company to rely on its belief that your particular injuries won't require extensive additional medical care, at least not $8,000 worth. It's a good compromise, and the mediation is successful.

---

**Mediation is very much an exercise in "compromise." Professional mediators are highly skilled at getting opposing parties to disengage from stubborn adherence to "win or lose" and focus instead on a "win/win" approach to conflict resolution. Mediation is *not* binding. Therefore, either party to mediation may turn to the courts if they're dissatisfied with the outcome.**

---

Mediation typically takes about a month from start to finish, and is an excellent alternative to protracted settlement negotiations or costly courthouse litigation. Another excellent reason to mediate is to avoid the physical, emotional, and psychological stress and strain of continued negotiation or litigation.

Many claimants choose mediation because of the relative guarantee of a quick and reasonable resolution of the claim without having to rehash all of the painful details and exhaustive documentation concerning the accident. Mediation is also advantageous because it allows the involved parties, not an outsider such as a judge, to determine the outcome of a claim.

With mediation, the parties to a conflict are brought together by the appointed mediator to identify and address those issues targeted for compromise. Mediation is non-confrontational by nature. It requires the full cooperation and participation of all parties to successfully reach an accord that is fair and acceptable to all. Mediation is a mutually cooperative and constructive alternative for conflict resolution that identifies and rectifies problems without causing additional damages or stresses to the participants.

## Litigation

Sometimes, certain aspects of a claim may make an early or uncomplicated insurance settlement unlikely or unwise, and may even preclude the possibility of arbitration or mediation. The insurance industry regularly reviews insurance claims. If your claim falls into any one of a number of different categories, your claim may automatically be headed for full-blown litigation before a judge and jury.

In some situations, because of circumstances completely beyond your control, there is nothing you can do to avoid litigation. No matter how diligently, reasonably, and responsibly you try to settle your case, the insurance company will refuse to settle. They'll insist on litigating your case before a judge and jury.

*In any event, it's usually not a good idea to purposefully hold out for a trial.*

If you find that your settlement negotiations are getting nowhere fast, call an attorney to arrange for a brief consultation. Perhaps your expectations for a settlement amount are too high. It's important to remember during your negotiations that it's not a "win/lose" situation. It's a compromise. And if you and the insurance company are failing to move closer to an acceptable compromise, it's time to try a different tactic. Often the assistance of an experienced personal injury attorney will get you pointed in the right direction toward a quick and fair settlement.

If you sense that your case is going to be litigated, you will need to decide if you're able to manage the demands and costs of *pro se* litigation. Time should be a determining factor in your decision. Because of the packed court calendars nationwide, the earliest available trial date may be two or three years in the future. Few people are able or willing to wait that long for reimbursement of their losses.

A "rule of thumb" that's true for any insurance claim: (1) try to negotiate; (2) if your negotiations aren't working, examine your strategy and make any changes that seem appropriate; and (3) if you're still not moving any closer to an acceptable compromise, hire a personal injury attorney.

## Litigation Costs

The high cost of litigation should always be considered. The costs of producing and managing all of the required records, subpoenas, depositions, court pleadings, professionally produced trial exhibits, and court appearances are high and escalating daily. It's not uncommon to see trial costs range from $5,000 to $15,000 or more. If you do decide to handle your own litigation, remember that the dollars will come from your pocket *before* any award is granted by a jury — dollars you may never recoup.

## Litigation Indicators

There are some "indicators" that an insurance company will vigorously look for and recognize when deciding if a case will be litigated. If your situation reflects any of these indicators, it's recommended that you seek the assistance of an attorney.

1. **Liability is contested.** You say it's his fault, and he says *you're* the one who caused the collision. Even worse, the

police reports are unclear as to who
caused the accident.

2. **Multiple parties are involved.** It's one
thing if you hit a telephone pole. It's quite
another if you're struck by a pick-up,
careen off an oncoming Volvo, take out a
parked station wagon, and land upside
down in a ditch. And it gets even more
complicated if other parties to the accident
were injured.

3. **There is another contributing cause.** Was
the road poorly designed? Did a construction crew leave debris in the middle of your
lane? Did a child rush into the street,
causing the car in front of you to swerve
and slam on the brakes? Any time something other than your own driving caused
your property damage and injury, the
insurance company will likely look to the
other potential sources of financial remu-
neration for your claim. As additional
parties are brought into your insurance
claim, and more people become concerned
with passing the financial burden onto
someone else, the chances of your case
making it all the way to litigation increase
dramatically.

4. **Property damage is low.** This is a red
alert for insurance companies! They're
looking for the minor fender bender that
produces a $10,000 injury claim. Cer-
tainly, seemingly minor impacts can cause

*If you sustain
injuries with no
or low property
damage, an early
legal consultation
is necessary.
Most insurance
companies are
forcing these
cases to trial.
Initial guidance
and preparation
are key to a fair
outcome.*

serious injuries. But unfortunately, some unscrupulous claimants have tried to get unreasonable settlements following such collisions. They've alerted the insurance industry to potential fraud in situations where minor property damage did not actually cause serious injuries.

5. **Significant injuries and/or damages, especially permanent injuries.** If you were seriously injured in an automobile accident, or if your injuries were permanent or disabling, the financial value of your claim increases. So too does the insurance company's desire to keep its money in its own bank accounts. The cost of litigation may well be worth the expense to an insurance company intent on *not* paying out a large settlement claim. A sure sign that litigation is forthcoming.

6. **Multiple accidents.** If you have a history of multiple accidents before the one you're negotiating now, your claim becomes more complicated. The insurance company may raise concerns that you're an irresponsible or dangerous driver, or that you're purposefully staging the accident to claim insurance money, or that any of your present claims for property damage or injury result from earlier accidents.

7. **Pre-existing conditions.** The validity of your claims becomes muddied by the existence of old injuries, especially if they

increase the pain or disability that you are presently claiming. Insurance companies are not eager to provide payments for old problems caused by drivers other than their insured. It is your responsibility to prove without a doubt that your pain and suffering were caused by the injuries received in the accident presently being litigated.

8. **Gaps in treatment.** If you didn't seek medical help immediately after the accident, or if you have long periods of time during which you didn't receive any medical care, the insurance company will question the seriousness of your claim and will fight tooth and nail before paying you a dime.

9. **Anything that looks like fraud.** Be truthful! Make reasonable and ethical demands. Just one little slip-up, and you'll find yourself in the courtroom facing a judge and jury who may be easily convinced that there's something fishy about your claim. They'll likely not believe any point of your case.

10. **The injured person doesn't present well.** It's a fact: if the jury doesn't like you as a person, you're probably not going to win. An abrasive personality, lack of good personal grooming, open hostility, a phony presentation — these personal quirks will help you to convince the jury, without any

help from the opposing side, that you don't deserve to win.

11. **The insurance company can detect a sense of urgency or desperation to settle.** The insurance company is going to wonder, *"What's the hurry here? What is this claimant afraid we'll discover?"* They'll likely do everything in their power to stall your claim all the way to the courthouse steps. If the insurance company senses that you're on the defensive, watch out!

12. **The plaintiff is *pro se*.** The average person, given the right tools and appropriate knowledge with sufficient time, temperament, and talent, can successfully negotiate and settle most insurance cases outside of the courtroom. However! The game changes once you step into that courtroom. The average person simply cannot compete with an experienced insurance litigator and the deep financial pockets of the insurance industry and mount a successful litigation offense and win.

13. **Excessive medical bills.** If your medical bills and expenses are disproportionately high relative to the nature of your injuries, you'd better be prepared to accept a settlement amount that is less than the actual medical costs you incurred. Otherwise, the insurance company will take you to court. It won't be difficult for them to

prove that you don't deserve full compensation for what they will depict as unreasonable and unnecessary medical costs.

14. **An insurance company that is more likely to litigate.** There's no way to predict when this might happen, because the list of insurance companies that are more likely to litigate changes over time. Remain aware throughout your settlement negotiations of the willingness of the insurance company to settle. If they're acting like hard-liners, then they probably *are* hard-liners, and will likely take you to court rather than ruin their coveted record of always settling low, or not at all.

15. **Self-employed with a large wage loss claim.** It's very difficult to accurately prove lost wages when you're self-employed. Insurance companies love to take full advantage of this fact. If you're self-employed, realize that your settlement negotiation battle is going to be a tough one. Unless you're willing to compromise or obtain professional legal help early on, you may end up in court.

16. **The injured person has unrealistic expectations as to the value of the claim.** Everyone wants full and reasonable compensation for property damage, injuries, and pain and suffering. Just what qualifies as "full" or "reasonable" is open to interpreta-

*If any of the litigation indicators apply to your case, a word to the wise: contact an experienced personal injury attorney immediately to handle the extremely demanding requirements and front the high costs of mounting a litigation effort.*

tion, depending on whose side you're on. But if you still haven't reached an acceptable compromise after diligent settlement negotiations with the insurance company, consider the possibility that you may be off-base in your expectations. If you're asking too much, the insurance company will simply refuse to move closer to your demand. In this case, it's time to obtain the qualified counsel of a personal injury attorney and find out if your demand is unreasonable and may be promoting an unpleasant ride straight to the courthouse.

Trial lawyers spend years and years learning how to best present a case and win it before a judge and jury. It is well beyond the scope of this book to provide you with an introduction to trial litigation. If your case is headed to a judge and jury, you will be doing yourself a tremendous disfavor if you opt to represent yourself in court.

## Summary

Now that you've learned everything you need to know to successfully negotiate an insurance claim on your own, we've provided a few recommended alternatives — arbitration or mediation — and reviewed an alternative that we don't recommend — courtroom litigation — in the event your best laid plans don't work out.

No matter how you decide to pursue your claim, you're going to make the entire experience much less stressful and far more successful if you remember that this isn't a "win or lose" proposition. You'll find professional and surprisingly cooperative individuals in the insurance industry who are just as interested as you are in settling your claim fairly and efficiently. If you should meet up with the few who don't share your reasonable approach to negotiation and settlement, you now have several alternatives that can keep you from hitting the wall of frustration and experiencing personal meltdown.

While the system of courtroom justice in our country is in many respects the envy of the world, it can be a confusing, frustrating, and heavily congested avenue to conflict resolution. If at all possible, learn how to successfully negotiate your claim and settle it without the added and unnecessary stress and strain of litigation.

If you've got the time, temperament, and talent, there's every reason to believe that you can manage successful negotiations that will proceed smoothly and efficiently.

Keep your sense of humor, follow the guidelines presented in this book, develop your own winning strategy, and know when to ask for help. If you follow these recommendations, you'll likely find that your settlement negotiations become an *enjoyable* exercise of your consumer rights.

Even more importantly, you'll discover that you dared to settle, *and won!*

# Survival Guide Checklist

☐ Consider mediation.

☐ Consider arbitration.

☐ Avoid litigation!

☐ Develop your own winning negotiation strategy.

☐ Know the litigation indicators that will send your case to trial.

☐ Know when to ask for help.

**NOTES**

# Index

# Index

# Index